Teach

Yourself

Cloth

Dollmaking

The Jodie DAVIS Needle Arts School

Teach

SIMPLE TECHNIQUES

Yourself

AND PATTERNS

Cloth

FOR DOLLS AND

Dollmaking

DOLL CLOTHES

JODIE DAVIS

PHOTOGRAPHY BY
BILL MILNE

FRIEDMAN/FAIRFAX
P U B L I S H E R S

A FRIEDMAN/FAIRFAX BOOK

Library of Congress Cataloging-in-Publication Data

Davis, Jodie, date
    Teach yourself dollmaking: simple techniques and patterns for
dolls and doll clothes / Jodie Davis.
        p.   cm.
            Includes index.
        ISBN 1-56799-159-9
        1. Dollmaking.   2. Doll clothes—Patterns.   3. Cloth dolls.
    I. Title.
    TT175.D384   1995
    745.592'21—dc20   94-5367
                                                                            CIP

Project Editor: Elizabeth Viscott Sullivan
Editor: Sharon Kalman
Art Director: Jeff Batzli
Designer: Tanya Ross-Hughes
Photography Director: Christopher C. Bain
Illustrator: Barbara Hennig
Production Associate: Camille Lee

Color separations by United South Sea Graphic Art Co., Ltd.
Printed in China by Leefung-Asco Printers Ltd.

For bulk purchases and special sales, please contact:
Friedman/Fairfax Publishers
Attention: Sales Department
15 West 26th Street
New York, NY 10010
212/685-6610   FAX 212/685-1307

dedication

To Lee Warhurst for sharing your half-full glass

acknowledgments

Thanks to the GEnie online quilters for unparalleled sisterhood, inspiration, and support.

Thanks to Jo-Ann Fabrics in Warrenton, Virginia, for having a sale that attracted a line at the cutting counter in which I met my good friend Barbara Hennig, the illustrator of this book.

Heartfelt thanks to Kathy Semone, for the gift of new perspective.

Thanks to my Mom, Anne Sullivan, for showing me I can.

Table of Contents

Introduction

Teach Yourself Cloth Dollmaking is a craft class in a book. Anyone possessing basic sewing skills can start with the first doll, and by the end of the book be an experienced dollmaker.

The idea for this book came from my friends on a nationwide computer bulletin board called GEnie. We were discussing the possibility of starting a local dollmaking class when a few onliners (computer bulletin board users) got the mistaken impression that we were planning to conduct this class online (on the computer). Why not?

As I completed each pattern in sequence I sent it out to dollmakers and soon-to-be dollmakers across the country. I instructed the participants to use the doll body pattern I sent, but to do whatever they fancied with hair, clothing, and accessories. The dolls they created are photographed throughout the book. I hope you will enjoy them and find that they spark your own creativity.

Since many of these dollmakers wanted to share their dollmaking tips, I have included many of them throughout the book.

the Magic of dollmaking

As with all classes, there are prerequisites for learning how to make these dolls. In this case: basic sewing skills

and the desire to create cloth dolls. As a bonus, dollmaking is a lot of fun!

Dollmaking does differ from garment sewing, though not in the obvious sense. The difference has nothing to do with stuffing, or jointing, or any other technique associated with dollmaking. Rather it's the magic you feel when you hold the doll out in front of you for the first time and begin to see a real personality emerge. These pieces of fabric you are sewing together are no longer merely inanimate objects.

What's wonderful about dollmaking is that no matter how carefully you trace the patterns, no matter how you attempt to replicate the materials I used, your doll will reflect your personality. This is what I want to share.

How to Use this book

I designed this book in a learn-as-you-go fashion. The first chapter covers a few of the basics you will need to know before you begin. I have provided basic equipment and supplies lists, dollmaking techniques you will increasingly rely on, and a few necessary background skills. All of this information is intended to make you feel confident in

tackling any cloth doll pattern.

Then you can jump right in by making the Basic Doll in Chapter Two. With this first pattern you will learn to mark, stitch, and cut out your doll, stuff it, clothe it in a simple dress, wig it with an easy hairstyle, and give it its own personality with a simple face.

Continuing on, you will find four more doll patterns, each requiring additional, and increasingly challenging, skills. The variations I have provided allow you to create a multitude of different dolls. My hope is that by the time you have finished the last chapter you will feel confident enough to try your hand at creating your own original dolls.

Don't forget to photograph, sign, and date each doll as you finish it. This way, you will have a chronology of all of your creations and you will see your progress with each doll.

So join my online friends in our dollmaking class. In no time we'll be sharing our first dolls with each other.

Jodie Davis

March 1994

Gainesville, VA

chapter 1

the

Basics

This chapter focuses on the basics of dollmaking: preparing patterns, preparing the fabric, and general information on creating faces and wigging a doll, both of which are covered in greater detail later in the book. Each chapter in this book provides all of the specific information you will need to create wonderful, unique dolls.

Dollmaking presents an opportunity to use all sorts of unique and unusual materials. Embellish clothing with colorful threads, woolly yarns, beads, buttons, lace, and fancy trims. Splurge on that scrumptious—and therefore expensive—fabric you've been eyeing: a doll's clothing requires only a mere fraction of a yard (meter).

Most of the equipment and supplies listed here are used in all of the dolls in this book. Many, if not all of these, can be found around the house. Some items are optional, such as the glue gun, and some are used only for specific dolls. Check the instructions for the specific doll you are making before you begin to determine exactly which supplies you'll need.

Equipment

Sewing machine
Machine needles appropriate for the fabric used
Dressmaker's shears
Paper scissors
Straight pins
Hand sewing needles
Long dollmaker's needle (see Sources, page 124)
Light table (optional)

Supplies

Air-soluble dressmaker's marking pen
Sewing thread
Quilting thread (for closing seams)
Waxed dental floss (for jointing)
Polyester fiberfill stuffing
Glue gun and glue sticks (optional)
White tacky glue
Fray Check™ seam sealant
Template material: cereal boxes, Mylar, or used file folders
#2 lead pencil
Unlined paper
Stuffing tools: Stuff-It™ (see Sources, page 124), chopsticks, wooden spoon, dowels of various sizes
Hemostats (for stuffing and turning; available at medical supply stores)

Preparing patterns

To use the doll and clothing patterns in this book, trace the patterns onto paper or use a copy machine. If you use a copy machine, be sure to first determine whether the machine copies accurately.

Some of the patterns were too big to fit on one page, so I cut these apart and placed them on adjacent pages. The number of parts needed to complete the pattern and the edges at which they should be joined are marked on the pieces. Follow the instructions below to use the pattern. An example is shown.

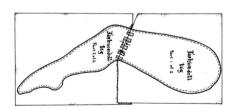

Cut out the pattern copies roughly, leaving extra paper outside the pattern lines. Glue the patterns to cereal boxes, Mylar, used file folders, or any material strong enough to withstand repeated use. With paper scissors, cut through both thicknesses along the outside edges of the pattern lines.

Preparing fabrics

To remove sizing and fabric finishes, prewash all fabrics used for your doll. If you won't be laundering the doll, it's not necessary to wash any unusual clothing fabrics.

face making

Creating faces is a personal matter, one which many dollmakers find to be the most challenging aspect of doll-making. Some dollmakers feel most comfortable with a needle, and therefore embroider. Others choose paint. Colored pencils, permanent pens—even crayons—are all commonly used. You may want to give all of these techniques a try before deciding which one you like best. As with any endeavor, practice will improve your skill.

I suggest you begin by practicing on scrap muslin. When you are ready to make the actual face, use the tip on page 18 to prepare the muslin for face making. Prepare several if you wish. When you've created one you like sew it into a finished doll. More detailed information on creating faces can be found on pages 107 to 111.

Following is a general list of the equipment and supplies you will need to make a doll's face. Each chapter in this book will include more specific materials.

Face-making supplies

Permanent fine-tip marking pens (I used Pigma Micron; see Sources, page 124)
Acrylic paints
Textile medium (found in fabric stores)
Paintbrushes of various sizes
Embroidery floss
Crayons
Colored pencils

Bonnie Lewis, Herndon, VA

Wigging Your doll

Let your imagination go wild when wigging your doll. From a simple braid of acrylic to fancy buns of mohair, yarn offers myriad possibilities. I often mix two, three, or more yarns for one doll's wig. Craft and fabric stores carry wool roving, curly crepe in a spectrum of hairlike colors, and synthetic ringlets. Explore the craft and floral departments of hobby stores for feathers and unusual fibers. Check the hardware store for natural hemp rope and jute twine. Dig into your scrap bag and tear muslin or colored and printed fabrics into strips for a rag doll's tresses. Rummage through your ribbon drawer or purchase curling ribbon. Bits of left-over fur fabric from toy-making projects are just the right touch for a toddler's or boy's wig. More detailed information on wigging your doll can be found on pages 39 to 43.

chapter 2

a

Basic

doll

For your introduction to dollmaking, I have designed a basic single-pattern-piece doll. The pattern is straightforward enough for a child to complete, yet it will teach you important techniques such as marking, stitching, turning, and stuffing that are necessary to create more sophisticated dolls.

Instructions for a basic face, easy hairstyle, and simple clothing will guide you quickly to a finished doll. If you prefer a more complicated face or wig, you'll find in-depth instructions elsewhere in the book. Refer to the index to find the information you need.

For a very easy clothing option, try "dressing" your doll in appliquéd clothing. Appliquéd clothing is applied before the doll is sewn together. I have provided instructions for an appliquéd leotard and bodysuit, though I encourage you to try your own ideas.

Don't let the simplicity of this doll fool you. One look at the spectrum of characters my dollmaking friends created from this one pattern shows what a little wizardry and ingenuity can conjure up.

I've drawn the pattern in two sizes: 4½ inches (11.5cm) and 9 inches (23cm). Try the larger size first; it's easier to work with. The smaller version makes an adorable pin-size doll. To wear your tiny creation, simply glue a pin back (found in any craft store) to the doll's back.

Finished sizes: Small: 4½ inches (11.5cm) tall; Large: 9 inches (23cm) tall

Materials

Body

   2 pieces of fabric, each 6 inches (15cm) square, for small doll

   2 pieces of fabric, each 10 by 11 inches (25 by 27cm), for large doll

#2 pencil or air-soluble marking pen

Matching thread

Polyester fiberfill stuffing

Yarn for hair

Clothing

Scraps of fabric for the top and skirt or pants

½ yard (45cm) of ribbon for the skirt tie

½ yard (45cm) of trim for the neck and armhole edges of the top

Instructions for a Basic doll

1 Prepare the patterns and fabric as instructed on pages 12 and 13.

2 Using a #2 pencil or an air-soluble marking pen, trace the doll pattern onto the wrong side of the body fabric. Align the arrow on the pattern with the lengthwise grain of the fabric (parallel to the selvedge—the lengthwise, uncut edge of the fabric).

3 Lay the pattern on a light table or tape it to a window. With the marked side down, align the marked fabric over the pattern. Trace the body outline and the face onto the right side of the fabric.

Place a piece of sandpaper under the fabric so it won't slide while you draw on it.
Linda Hershfield, Flushing, NY

4 Lay the marked fabric right side down on a second piece of body fabric which is right side up. Pin the layers together. (Main doll instructions continue on page 18.)

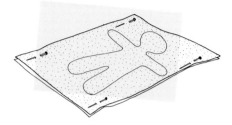

appliqued Clothing

Layers of fabric and a machine satin stitch make appliquéd clothing an easy doll-dressing alternative. Here is your opportunity to use those special fabric scraps and fancy threads you've been saving.

Jodie Davis, Gainesville, VA

Materials

Scraps of fabric for bodysuit and leotard Decorative thread (I used Madeira Metallic; see Sources, page 124)

1 Prepare one piece of body fabric as instructed in steps 2 and 3, page 16. Trace the body outline onto the wrong side of a second piece of body fabric. Transfer the clothing markings to the wrong sides of both body pieces.

2 Cut each of the bodysuit and leotard fabrics into two pieces, each large enough to cover the doll generously. Lay one leotard piece right side down. Lay one bodysuit piece right side down on top. With the marked side down, lay one body piece on top. Repeat for

the remaining bodysuit, leotard, and body piece. Pin. Straight stitch along the marked leotard clothing lines. Trim the clothing to the stitching.

3 Using decorative thread, machine satin stitch over the previously stitched lines on the right side of the front and back of the doll.

4 Pin the two body pieces together, right sides facing, matching the body outline markings. Continue on to step 5 of the main doll instructions (page 18).

Some dollmakers prefer to make their doll's faces before stitching the doll. As Sandy Anderson of Woodbury, MN, says, "If I make a truly horrendous face I can scrap it right then and start over. This is much less frustrating than messing up the face on a doll that I've already stitched and stuffed."

"I recommend embroidering the face before cutting the fabric and sewing the doll. It is amazing how much easier it is!"
Donna Murray, South St. Paul, MN

4 "Instead of making a template and tracing around it, trace the pattern directly from the book onto freezer paper. Trace the face and other markings onto the freezer paper. Iron the marked freezer paper onto the wrong side of the prepared fabric. Hold the fabric/pattern up to a light source, such as a window, having the freezer paper against the window. Trace the face placement onto the right side of the fabric with a black or brown permanent pen, such as a Pigma [see Sources, page 124].

Paint, embroider, or otherwise add the features to the face.

Lay the fabric/pattern face down on a second piece of fabric which is right side up. Continue on to step 5. After stitching, tear the freezer paper away from the fabric."

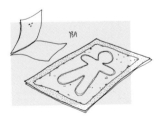

Sandy Anderson, Woodbury, MN; Joan Fearing, St. Paul, MN; Linda Schiffer, Columbia, MD

5 (Continued from page 17) Set your machine to a slightly shortened stitch, about sixteen stitches per inch (2.5cm). This will make a stronger and smoother seam, and since the stitches will be smaller, it will be easier to stitch around curves and into points accurately.

6 Backstitch to secure the beginning of the seam, then stitch just inside the traced lines. When you sew tight curves, such as at the neck, you may have to stop after each stitch to lift the presser foot and turn the fabric slightly. Take one stitch straight across the body at the crotch.

7 Stop stitching about ¾ inch (2cm) for the small doll or 2 inches (5cm) for the large doll before you reach the beginning of the stitching. Backstitch at the end of the stitching.

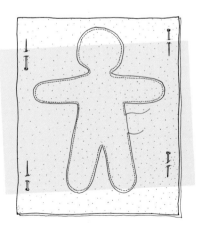

Denise Rominger, Cranbury, NJ

If your sewing machine is equipped with an open-toe embroidery foot, try using it when stitching your doll. You will be able to see the marked line as you sew along it and following the line will be much easier.

To make the seams stronger, stitch again on top of the first stitching. This will help prevent the seams from popping when you stuff the doll.

Trimming & clipping Seams

"For an alternative opening, stitch all the way around the marked line. Overlap the beginning and end of the stitching. To turn this doll right side out cut a slash in one layer of the doll in an area of her body which will be covered with clothing or hair."

Brenda Groelz, Phillips, NE; Evelyn Portrait, Lynn, MA

8 Trim the seam allowance to ⅛ inch (3mm), except at the unstitched opening: trim this to ¼ inch (6mm). Clip into the curve at the neck and to the straight stitch between the legs.

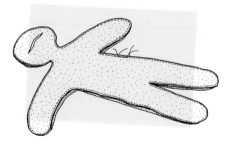

After stitching the doll, I trim the seam allowance to ⅛ inch (3mm). Deeper seam allowances will not allow the fabric to give when turned and stuffed, which will cause it to pucker. Judicious clipping of seam allowances helps, but tends to create a bumpy appearance on the finished doll. I found that trimming the seams to ⅛ inch gives a smooth, finished appearance. With this method I don't need to clip every curve, only sharp curves such as at the neck, and V's such as those between the fingers.

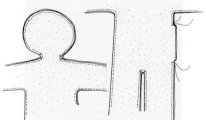

A drop of Fray Check™ at these clips will prevent them from raveling. Do be careful with this product, though. On some fabrics it will show, even when dry, so keep it in the seam allowances. It likes to migrate, so use just a drop.

A ¼-inch (6mm) seam allowance at the unstitched opening affords more fabric for ladderstitching the opening after stuffing the doll. To prevent fraying when ladderstitching, apply Fray Check to the raw edges of these seam allowances.

It may be helpful when you stitch the opening closed later to mark the stitching line at the opening now (so you will be able to see it later). Do so on the right sides of the fabric—those facing one another.

"I like to trim the seam allowance outside the stitching line with pinking shears. This method helps the fabric turn around the curves better when I turn the body right side out."

Linda Schiffer, Columbia, MD

9 Turn the doll right side out.

10 Stuff the doll (see instructions on page 20), beginning with the legs. Then stuff the head, neck, and arms. Finish by stuffing the torso. (Main doll instructions continue on page 21.)

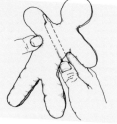

"To smooth the seam and give a crisp, even, finished look, insert a pointed tool such as a Stuff-It™ or a chopstitck into the doll. Run it along the seam to push it out fully and smoothly."

Judy Rogers, Medina, OH

Stuffing

As with most skills, stuffing is a learned art. For best results start with high-quality stuffing, since inferior products often lump in the doll. Quality stuffing is resilient and will remain uniform in texture, even after pieces of varying sizes are stuffed into the doll. Quality stuffing costs a bit more, but it is a small price to pay for an easily and evenly stuffed doll. Currently, Fairfield's Soft Touch Polyfil Supreme and Airtex are my favorite stuffings.

Stuffing tools may be as close as your workshop or kitchen. Cut a dowel 6 to 10 inches (15 to 25cm) long. Sand one end of the dowel smooth, and give the other end a point in a pencil sharpener. Sand the point smooth. For larger dolls, the handle end of a wooden spoon works well. A chopstick is a favorite of many dollmakers. The Stuff-It™ tool has a rounded end that glides easily inside the turned doll body to smooth the seams.

Begin by stuffing the smallest part of the section you are stuffing first. For example, if you are stuffing the legs, begin with the toes. For a single-pattern-piece doll, stuff the legs, then the head, neck, arms, and finally the torso, working toward the unstitched opening.

Size the pieces of fiberfill to the area being stuffed. For the arms and legs of a 9-inch (23cm) doll I use pieces about the size of a nickel. By the time I get to the body I use walnut-size pieces. For comparison, the fingers of the fashion doll (page 102) require mere wisps of stuffing, each pushed in one at a time.

Using your stuffing tool, push the stuffing firmly into the doll. It should stay in place when you remove the tool. After you add a few more pieces, check to be sure that the first piece of stuffing is still firmly in place, filling out the fabric smoothly and fully.

It's easy to end up with a wobbly neck, so take special care around this area. Even if you stuff the rest of the doll softly for a cuddly child's toy, stuff the neck area well, including the base of the head and the top of the shoulders.

Aim for symmetry. If you reach the shoulder, and realize the arm you just stuffed is more softly stuffed than the other arm, unstuff the second arm and start over. You can add a small amount of stuffing to a specific spot by sliding the stuffing under the "skin" of the doll. This will work successfully only with a high-quality, non-lumping stuffing.

Mary Ellen Foster, Lakewood, CO

"When I stuffed Autumn, the doll I made from this basic doll pattern, I accidentally grabbed a bag of old stuffing from my closet. I couldn't figure out why the arms and legs were so lumpy. I ended up stuffing the doll so full that one of the seams burst. This has never happened before. Then I read the label and realized I was using the wrong stuffing."

Madeline Molis, Rancho Palos, CA

To stuff large areas such as the torso, stuff as if you were lining a bowl with lady fingers. Stuff the bottom, then begin working up the sides. Add more stuffing to the bottom. Continue to stuff, pushing the fiberfill toward the outside of the doll. For a larger doll you may use your fingers for this; otherwise use a stuffing tool. When you fill the body up to the side opening, stuff the top of the torso. Continue stuffing the torso, working back toward the opening. If after you stuff the torso you find it isn't firm enough, push the stuffing already in the torso out toward the edges and add more stuffing to the inside of the doll.

Stuffing takes patience and time. If you're not happy with your stuffing job, unstuff and try again. With practice, you will improve.

11 (Continued from page 19.) Ladderstitch the gap in the stitching at the side of the doll closed or whipstitch the slash in the body.

Closing body Seam Openings

ladderstitch

For a virtually invisible seam closure, use the ladderstitch.

Knot the end of a single strand of quilting thread or dental floss or a double strand of sewing thread. From inside the doll, push the needle up through the fabric about ¼ inch (6mm) below one end of the opening.

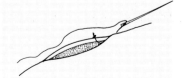

Go into the fabric close to where you came out. Come up about ⅛ inch (3mm) closer to the opening.

Take a stitch measuring about ⅛ inch (3mm) along the seamline on one side of the seam.

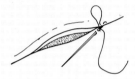

Cross over to the other side of the opening and take another ⅛-inch (3mm) -long stitch along the seamline, about ⅛ inch further along the opening.

Continue taking stitches from alternate sides, working your way along the opening. Pull up on the stitches as you go. When you reach the end of the opening, make a knot. Push the needle into the fabric close to the knot and emerge somewhere in the fabric. Pull the thread tight, then trim the end close to the fabric.

Whipstitch

If you slashed an opening to turn your doll, use the whipstitch to close it.

Knot the end of a single strand of quilting thread or dental floss or a double strand of sewing thread.

Push the needle into the fabric on one side of one end of the slash. Emerge at the other side of the slash.

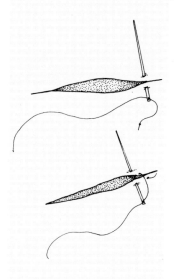

Repeat along the slash, making the stitches ⅛ to ¼ inch (3 to 6mm) apart. When you reach the end of the slash, knot the thread and trim the end.

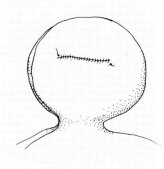

the Face

Once you have completed the doll's body you can begin to work on the face. For more detailed information on creating doll faces, see pages 107 to 111.

1 Using a fine-tip permanent marker, draw the eyelids and mouth.

2 Using paints, crayons, or markers, color the lips within the lines.

3 For the eyes: If using paints, paint the whites of the eyes. Set aside to dry. Paint the iris brown, blue, or a color of your choice. Allow to dry. With the tip of your brush, make a black pupil at the center of the eye. This can be small or large. Let dry. Add a tiny dot of white to each pupil. If using

Susan Holman, Laytonsville, MD

markers or crayons, draw in the pupil first, leaving an empty space for the white highlight of the eye. Draw the iris around the pupil, using the desired color.

4 Paint or draw the eyebrows, eyelashes, and nose.

"To add the white highlight dot to the pupil, dip the tip of a toothpick or the blunt end of an unfolded paper clip into white paint. Gently apply a dot of paint to one outside edge of each pupil at two or ten o'clock."

Linda Hargan,
Elk Grove, CA

"Use a pencil point and white correction fluid for the whites of the doll's eyes."

Patti Welsh,
Morrison, CO

Jodie Davis, Gainesville, VA

Hair

~~~~~~~~~~

Below are instructions for a basic doll wig. For more detailed information on finding unique materials for wigs and on wigging your doll, turn to pages 39 to 43.

1 Measure the doll as shown to determine how long you want to make the hair.

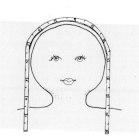

2 Loop the yarn as shown. To determine how much yarn to use, pick the yarn up at the center and hold it on the doll's head.

3 Using a piece of the yarn, tie the center of the yarn together.

4 Stitch tie to the head.

5 Trim the ends of the yarn as desired. To keep the hair in place, apply glue to the doll's head. If the glue is too thick, thin with water. Press the yarn to the head. This will secure the under layer, especially important around the face.

Clothing

I have provided instructions for clothing to fit the large doll. The small doll is too little to dress in this manner.

Diane Roode Schneck, New York, NY

top

1 Right sides together, pin the two top pieces together at the sides and shoulders. Stitch.

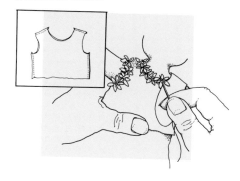

2 Put the top on the doll. Handstitch the trim over the raw edges.

skirt

1 Cut a piece of fabric 4 by 12 inches (23 by 30cm). Right sides together, stitch the short ends together.

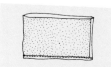

2 Press one long edge ¼ inch (6mm) to the wrong side. Repeat. Topstitch. This will be the hem edge.

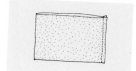

3 Press the top edge ¼ inch (6mm) to the wrong side. Gather this edge by hand or machine. Put the skirt on the doll. Pull up on the gathering to fit. Knot the thread ends, then trim.

4 Tie a piece of ribbon around the doll's waist, concealing the gathered edge of the fabric. Trim the ribbon ends.

pants

1 Right sides together, fold each pant leg to match inseam edges. Stitch.

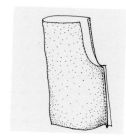

2 Turn one leg right side out and slip inside the second leg. Match seams at crotch. Stitch. Turn right side out.

3 At the lower edge of each pant leg press ¼ inch (6mm) to the wrong side. Repeat. Topstitch the folded edge.

4 Press ¼ inch (6mm) to the wrong side along the waist edge. Repeat. Gather this edge by hand or machine. Put the pants on the doll. Pull up on the gathering to fit. Knot the thread ends, then trim.

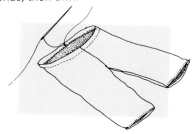

5 Tie a piece of ribbon around the doll's waist, concealing the gathered top of the pants. Trim the ribbon ends.

Linda Hargan, Elk Grove, CA

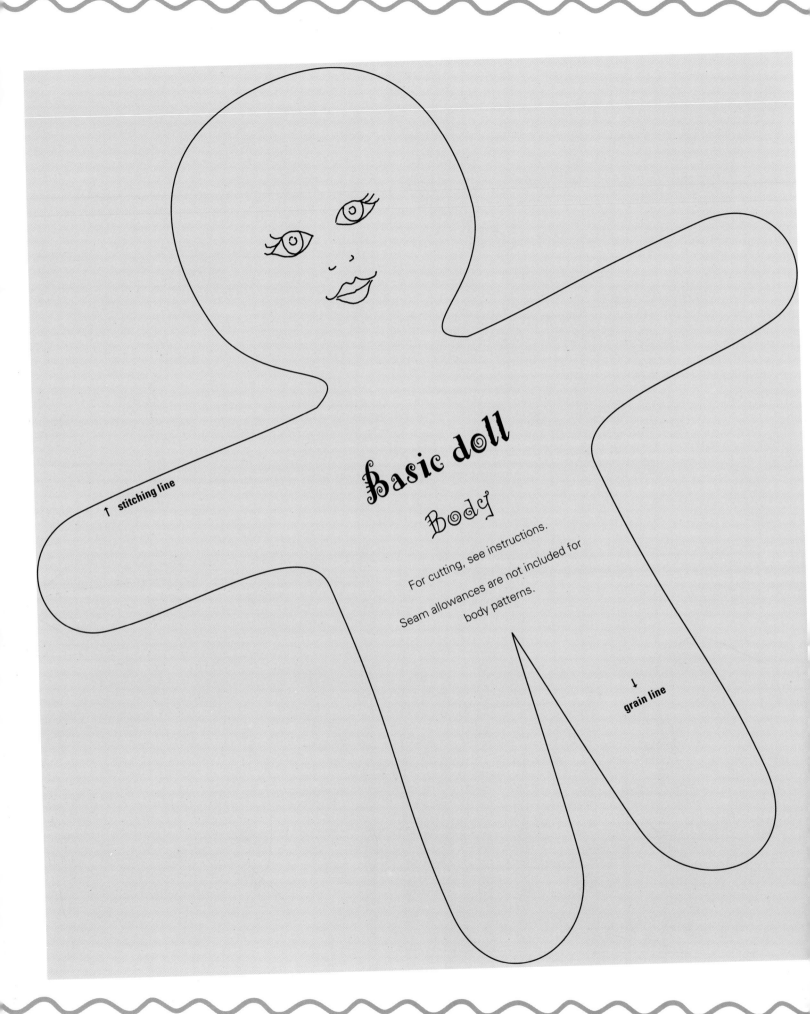

↑ **stitching line**

Basic doll

Body

For cutting, see instructions.

Seam allowances are not included for body patterns.

↓
grain line

Basic doll

Top

↓
grain line

Cut 2

Basic doll

Pants

↑ Place on fold ↑

↑ crotch

↑ inseam

↓
grain line

Cut 2

Pin doll

Seam allowances are
not included for
body patterns.

↓
grain line

chapter 3

Pancake doll

Add to your dollmaking skills with a second single-pattern-piece doll. Learn to use an armature to give your doll the ability to pose and stand on her own two feet, or stitch joints so your doll can sit and bend her arms. Give your doll fingers with an easy topstitching technique. If you choose, forego painting or embroidery; appliqué stuffed fabric features to your doll's face.

You can make this doll with or without the armature. Without one, you can stitch joint the doll, but it is not necessary. Refer to the sources (page 124) to find a supplier of premade armatures or to chapter 6 (page 96) for instructions on making your own. Instructions are given here for an armature protruding from the bottom of the doll's legs for insertion into a base and for an armature that is totally enclosed inside the doll, making her poseable but not attachable to a base. Stuffing is more time-consuming and trickier with the armature, but posing the finished doll is lots of fun. What a thrill when she stands on her own!

Finished size: 16 inches (40cm) tall

Materials

Body

$^5/_8$ yard (57cm) of fabric for the doll body

Matching thread

Polyester fiberfill stuffing

2 skeins of yarn for hair (I used $^1/_4$ pound (113g) of Copper Natural Wave from Fleece and Unicorn; see Sources, page 124)

Matching thread

Paint, markers, crayons, or embroidery floss for face (omit for appliquéd face)

Armature (optional)

Wooden stand (if using non-enclosed armature)

Clothing

$^1/_2$ yard (45cm) of fabric for dress

Matching thread

12 inches (30cm) of $^1/_8$-inch (3mm) -wide elastic

$3^1/_2$- by 5-inch (9 by 12.5cm) scrap of fabric for apron

15- by 20-inch (37.5 by 50cm) piece of fabric for cape (I used a loosely woven wool so that I could fringe the edges)

$^5/_8$ yard (57cm) of $1^1/_4$-inch (3cm) -wide ribbon

16-inch (40cm) square of fabric for kerchief

Scrap of fabric for shoes—synthetic suede or suedelike fabric

10 tiny buttons or beads for shoe buttons

Instructions for Pancake doll

1 Prepare the patterns as instructed on pages 12 and 13.

2 Trace the face and body outline pattern onto the fabric as instructed in steps 2 through 4, pages 16 and 17.

3 Stitch the two layers of fabric, right sides together, just inside the marked lines. If using an armature and a stand, stitch all the way around, overlapping the beginning and end of the stitching about ½ inch (12mm). (In step 6 [page 31] you will slash the doll's body at center back to insert the armature and stuff the doll.) If not using an armature, either leave a 2-inch (5cm) gap in the stitching along one side of the doll's torso, or use the slashing method in step 6 as for the doll with the armature. Trim the seam allowance to ⅛ inch (3mm).

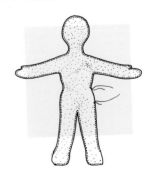

4 If using an armature, transfer the dots on the bottoms of the feet to the body back piece. Make holes through the fabric large enough for the wire of the armature to slip through. Apply Fray Check to the raw edges of the holes.

5 Transfer the ankle dart marking to the front of the legs. To create the bend at the ankle, crease the fabric at the dart on each leg, then stitch along the marked line.

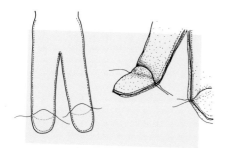

6 If the doll will be turned through a slash, make a 3-inch (7cm) -long slash at the center back (the side without the ankle darts) of the doll. Clip the seam allowance at the neck. Apply Fray Check to raw edges of slash and clips. Allow to dry.

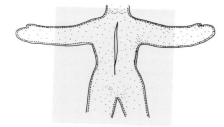

7 Trim seam allowances at fingers to approximately 1/16 inch (1.5mm). Clip the seam allowance between fingers, between thumb and hand, and at neck. Carefully clip between the two lines of stitching at the crotch. Apply Fray Check to all of these raw edges. While Fray Check is still wet, turn the doll right side out.

"I was making a doll and the only part that wasn't working was the neck. So I inserted my stuffing tool (my trusty chopstick) and just left it there. I continued to stuff with

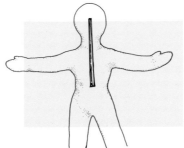

another chopstick. It worked like a charm. I added lots of long curly hair to this doll and her neck didn't budge. The chopstick runs all the way from the top of the head to about the middle of the torso, so it's quite sturdy!"

Donna Murray, South St. Paul, MN

8 To stuff the doll without an armature, turn to the instructions on page 20.
(Doll instructions continue on page 32.)

To avoid a wobbly neck on your doll try these suggestions: "For a small doll, hot glue two coffee straws at top and bottom. For a larger doll, recycle an empty waxed paper roll and cut to desired length."

Kathy Semone, Silver Spring, MD

"I have been known to insert a pencil or dowel from the chest area up to ear level. This has helped greatly."

Judy Rogers, Medina, OH

"A paint stir stick from the hardware store works well, as do tongue depressors."

Marcia Spencer, Delevan, NY

Stitched joints

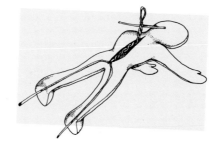

On a doll without an armature you can quickly and easily add bendable joints at the elbows, knees, and hips. For the knee, stuff the leg from the foot to about ½ inch (12mm) below the marked lines at the knee. Topstitch across the leg along the marked line. A zipper foot will allow you to stitch close to the stuffing.

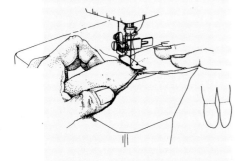

Continue to stuff up to about ¾ inch (2cm) below the top of the leg. Topstitch along the marked line. Do the same for the elbows.

9 (Continued from page 31.) To stuff the doll with an armature and a stand: stuff the toes and foot almost as far as the hole in the bottom of the foot. Insert the long leg wires into the legs and out through the holes at the bottoms of the feet.

10 Stuff the remainder of the foot, ankle, and leg. For an armature that is enveloped inside the body, position the armature over the doll as it would be inside the doll. Bend the leg wires up so that the bend is just above the ankle. Twist the free end of the wire around the leg wire. Trim the excess wire. Insert the armature into the doll's legs. To stuff around the wire, push a piece of stuffing down one side of the wire and work into place. Push another piece of stuffing down the other side of the wire. Continue in this manner, keeping the wire in the center of the stuffing. Stuff the legs and hips almost up to the waist.

11 Stuff the top two thirds of the head. Stuff the fingers, hands, and wrists.

12 Insert one arm wire into one side of the shoulder piece and push it halfway inside. Bend the wire at the forearm. Twist it around itself. Trim the

Bonnie Lewis, Herndon, VA

tip of the wire flush with the wire it's twisted around. Insert into the doll's arm. Repeat for the remaining arm.

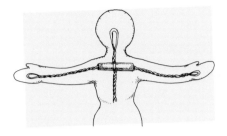

You may have to bend the backbone of the armature to get the arm wire into the doll body. Insert the neck stem into the head.

13 Stuff the arms, beginning at the wrist. Add stuffing around the wire, enveloping the wire in stuffing. Continue to stuff the arm.

14 Finish stuffing the head, encasing the wire in the center of the head with fiberfill. Stuff the neck, the shoulders, and then the remainder of the torso.

15 Stuff the fingers and toes lightly. Topstitch by hand or machine along the marked lines, backstitching at the beginning and ends of the stitching, then continue stuffing.

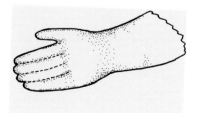

16 For the doll with an armature, whipstitch the slashed opening closed (see page 21). If you left an opening at the doll's side, ladderstitch closed (see page 21).

17 Add the face on the doll as directed on pages 107 to 111, or refer to the following instructions for an appliquéd face.

Appliquéd Face

Appliqué is an easy technique for creating a face, especially for those who are handier with a needle than with a brush or pen. This is an easy technique as all of the shapes are provided here. For the nose and eyelids use the same fabric you used for the head. Use red fabric for the mouth, and blue or brown fabric for the eyes.

1 For each appliqué: fold the fabric so the right sides are together. Trace the appliqué pattern onto the fabric. Stitch all the way around just inside the marked lines. Overlap the beginning and end of the stitching.

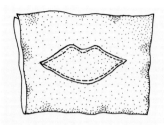

2 Trim the seam allowance to ⅛ inch (3mm). Apply Fray Check. Make a slash through the marked fabric layer.

Turn right side out.

3 Insert a small amount of stuffing to pad the fullness of the lips. Stitch the lip line on the mouth using red thread, then appliqué the lips to the doll's face with a backstitch or slip stitch.

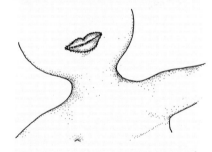

4 The nose needs a bit more stuffing than the lips. When it is stuffed, indent it at the bottom side as you stitch it to the face.

Jodie Davis, Gainesville, VA

Jodie Davis, Gainesville, VA

6 Slipstitch the eye appliqué to the face, following the pattern markings. Position the lid so that it bows out over the eye.

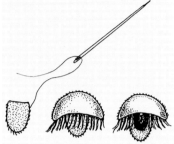

For the pupil, stitch a black bead or button to the iris, or paint or draw a pupil with black paint or permanent marker. Draw in eyebrows, if desired.

hair

Detailed information on wigging a doll is found later in this chapter, on pages 39 to 43.

1 Draw a 4-inch (10cm) -long line on a piece of paper. Lay a hank of yarn across the center of the line.

2 With matching thread, machine stitch along the line through the paper and yarn. Backstitch at the beginning and end of the stitching. Stitch again over the previous stitching.

5 For eyelashes, cut a piece of tape approximately ⅛ by ½ inch (3 by 12mm). Adhere the ends of ½-inch-long pieces of black embroidery floss to the length of the tape. Glue the tape to the back of the eyelid.

3 Tear away the paper and place the hair on the doll's head so that the stitching forms a "part." Fold under

the first ½ inch (12mm) of the hair at the front of the doll's head. Hand stitch along the "part" to attach the hair to the head. Trim the ends of the hair.

4 Beginning at the "part," roll the first inch or two (about 2.5 to 5cm) of yarn at the front of the hair toward the back.

5 Add the next 1- or 2-inch (2.5 or 5cm) -long section of hair to the roll, and then another. Using a scrap of yarn, tie the roll at about ear height.

Dress

Note: All seam allowances are ¼ inch (6mm) unless otherwise specified.

1 Prepare patterns and fabrics as instructed on pages 12 and 13. Cut two 4- by 5-inch (10 by 12.5cm)

Jodie Davis, Gainesville, VA

rectangles for the sleeves. Cut a 17- by 18-inch (42.5 by 45cm) rectangle for the skirt.

2 Right sides together, match and stitch the shoulder seams of one bodice front to two bodice backs. Repeat for the lining pieces.

3 Right sides together, pin the neck and back edges of the bodice and bodice lining together. Stitch. Turn right side out. Press.

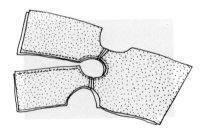

4 Right sides together, and treating the two layers of the bodice as one, pin and stitch one short edge of a sleeve to the bodice.

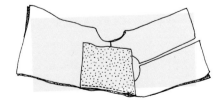

Repeat for the remaining sleeve.

5 Right sides together, stitch side and sleeve seams as one.

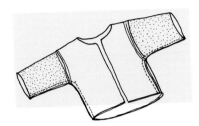

6 Press ¼ inch (6mm) to the wrong side twice along one short edge of the apron piece. Repeat. Then repeat for each long side. Topstitch the folded edges.

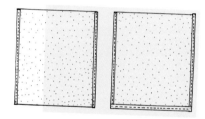

7 Right sides together, stitch the short edges of the dress skirt together. Use a long basting stitch halfway, backstitch, then continue with a regular stitch.

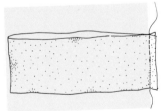

8 Press the seam open. Topstitch ⅛ inch (3mm) along basted portion of the seam down one side, across and up the other side. Remove basting stitches. This opening will be the waist edge of the skirt.

9 Press ¼ inch (6mm) to the wrong side on the raw hem edge of the skirt. Fold again and press. Topstitch.

10 Gather the remaining raw edge of the skirt.

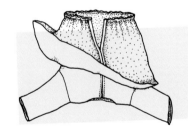

11 Pin the center front of the apron to the center front of the skirt. With the right sides together, pin the raw edges of the bodice to the skirt, sandwiching the apron between the layers and adjusting gathers to fit. Stitch the skirt to the bodice.

12 Press ¼ inch (6mm) to the wrong side at the lower edge of each sleeve. Repeat. Topstitch a scant ¼ inch from the pressed edge, leaving a ¼-inch opening in the stitching. Thread a darning needle with about 20 inches (50cm) of doubled dental floss. Tie the dental floss to a 6-inch (15cm) length of the elastic. With the eye first, run the needle through the casing. Bring the needle out,

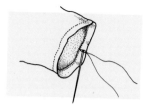

dle out, pulling the elastic through. Remove the dental floss. Repeat this

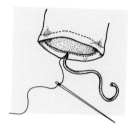

procedure for the second sleeve. Put the dress on the doll. Adjust the elastic and knot ends. If desired, sew a snap or hook and loop fastener to back neck of dress.

Cape

1 Stitch ½ inch (12mm) from the raw edge along all sides of the cape piece. Use a pin to pull threads from along all raw edges to fringe them.

2 Fold one 15-inch (37.5cm) edge 3 inches (7cm) to the wrong side.

Topstitch ½ inch (12mm) from the fold to make a casing. Attach a safety pin to one end of the ribbon. Insert pin into casing and pull through.

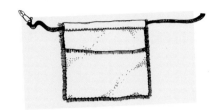

3 Remove the pin. Pull up on the ribbon to gather the cape as much as possible. Knot each end of the ribbon to secure the gathers. Put the cape on

the doll and tie the ribbon into a bow at the doll's neck.

Kerchief

1 Stitch ½ inch (12mm) from all edges of the kerchief piece.

2 Fringe all edges as for cape.

3 Fold the kerchief in half diagonally to form a triangle. Tie around the doll's head as shown.

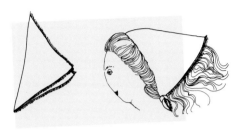

Shoes

1 Match two shoe pieces, right sides together. For a doll without an armature, stitch from the top of the shoe at front, down and around the toe and up to the back top, leaving the straight edges on top open. Trim seam allowance to ⅛ inch (3mm). Turn right side out. Put on the doll.

If your doll has an armature, stitch from the top of the shoe, down the front and along the toe. Stop at the dot.

Trim seam allowance around the toe to ⅛ inch (3mm). Turn right side out.

2 Put the shoes on the doll. For the armatured doll, ladderstitch (see page 21) the remaining open section of the shoe, having the armature wire extend from the seam just where you stopped stitching.

3 Stitch five black buttons or beads to the side of each shoe.

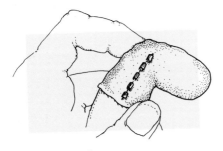

Armature Stand

Denise Rominger, Cranbury, NJ

Note: Premade finished or unfinished wooden bases are available at craft stores. I used a block of oak I found in our barn to make a stand.

1 Drill two holes in the stand, using a drill bit slightly smaller than the wire. I placed the holes about 1¾ inches (4.5cm) apart. Depending upon the pose you wish your doll to take, you may choose another distance, perhaps to create a walking effect.

2 Trim the armature wire almost long enough to reach the bottoms of the holes when the doll is placed upon the stand. Put the doll on the stand and insert the wires into the holes. Pose the doll as desired.

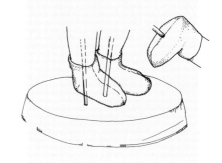

Doll hair

Doll hair options are limited only by your imagination. Nearly every craft store carries curly crepe, yarns ranging from common acrylics to specially packaged doll hair, Santa beard yarn, and curly synthetics in a variety of colors. Craft fur works well for boy and baby hair.

Evelyn Portrait, Lynn, MA

Yarn, the obvious choice, offers all sorts of textures from the uniformity of cotton strands to the fuzzy softness of mohair. A trip to a yarn shop will reveal many exciting possibilities. Metallic yarns can be used alone or mixed with nonmetallic yarn. There are even yarns that have tiny pieces of fabric woven into them. I like to mix two or more different yarns for doll hair. This way I can add a hint of metallic gleam to an angel's golden hair, add a touch of purple to an otherwise all-black witch's wig, or create a more realistic sun-bleached look with two shades and textures of blonde yarn.

Natural hair materials include mohair and wool yarns, flax, excelsior, feathers, and even dried flowers. Dried or silk flowers, especially roses, hot-glued around a doll's face and the back of her head make a lovely spring

"In the past, my favorite hair has been made of fabric. My first cloth doll had hair made from a whole bunch of fabric selvedges in all colors. I just tacked these to the doll's head piece by piece until the scalp was covered.

Another doll has hair made of ⅛-inch [3mm] -wide satin ribbon that stands straight up. My favorite hair so far is on a doll I made as a Christmas gift for a friend who sometimes wears her hair in corn row braids. To duplicate it, I made a wig of thin twisted black satin fringe. I couldn't figure out how to cover the entire head, so I glued on a hat. The braids stick out from under the hat."

Diane Schreck, New York, NY

"My doll's wings are made from a patchwork print, so I figured she needed hair to go along with the quilting theme. I got the idea of what to use for her hair while trimming the threads off a 1930s quilt top. All the colors of thread—when balled up—became a wig for my little gal. I covered her head with craft glue and just stuck a ball of thread to the doll's head with glue."

Patti Porter, Cincinnati, OH

bonnet of hair. Torn strips of fabric are the perfect crown for a country rag doll. If you wish, rotary cut the strips for a less frayed look. Try tea-dyed muslin, black or brown cotton fabric, multiple fabrics, or even printed fabric for your doll's hair.

Melanie Dailey, Delevan, NJ

"I used blue tinsel for the hair of my Mermaid doll. I just took the tinsel out of the bag, taped down the middle of one side of it, sewed a straight line down the tape, flipped the tinsel over, and hot-glued it to the head!"

Donna Murray, St. Paul, MN

Dig into your ribbon and trim stash for more wigging materials. Use curling ribbon or sew loops of ribbon to the doll's head. Embroidery floss, perle cotton, or yarn can be glued to the doll's head for a slick hairdo. For an unusual look, glue a stainless steel cleaning pad to your doll's head. Leave it wound up or clip the coils so they hang.

I've heard of dollmakers using strips cut from pantyhose, paper clips, coiled colored wire gleaned from telephone cable, and even cut-up plastic bags for their doll's hair.

Keep your eyes open. You never know what will say "doll hair" to you!

"I collect and mix any number of fringe, eyelash, multi-textured, multi-fibered (sometimes unraveled), metallic, cotton and mohair yarns, ribbons, cords, and nearly anything that suits my fancy. For two dolls for friends I looped a feather boa down and back up for ponytails."

Karla Newsome, Westminster, CO

"I treated my doll's hair like a wig. I crocheted a cap and then 'hooked' strands of yarn through the cap. When it was all finished I just glued it to her head."

Evelyn Portrait, Lynn, MA

Pat Shaw, Birmingham, AL

Wig techniques

Yarn

A very versatile doll hair material, yarn can be manipulated into many different looks.

basic Wig

For a basic wig with a center "part," decide where you want the hair "part" to start on the forehead. Measure back to about the center back of the head for a free-falling hairstyle, all the way to the neck for two ponytails or braids. Draw a line of this length on a piece of paper.

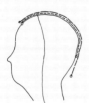

Measure the doll as shown to determine the length of hair you desire. If making braids for your doll then add at least half again as much.

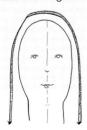

Wind yarn in loops this length to fill the line on the paper. Machine stitch the center of the loops to the paper, backstitching at the beginning and end of the stitching.

Tear one side and then the other of the paper from the stitching. Place the wig on the doll's head. Hand stitch the "part" to the head.

You may stitch the yarn to a piece of muslin rather than paper. Once it is stitched, trim the muslin along the stitching and glue it to the doll's head.

Margarita Wilcox, Auburn, CA

You can now braid the yarn in one or two braids, tie it in one or two ponytails, or leave it hanging free.

To add bangs, measure across the doll's forehead. Draw a line this length on a piece of paper. Stitch looped yarn to this line on the paper. Tear away the paper. Hand stitch the machine stitching to the doll's forehead. You may find it easier to stitch the bangs in place before adding the remaining hair.

Hairline Method

For a bun or any upswept or pulled back hairstyle, first decide where you want the hairline and draw it lightly on the doll. Measure along this line from the center of the forehead around to the center back of the head. Draw a

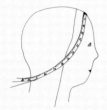

line this length on paper. Stitch the center of the yarn, looped to the desired length, to the line. Remove the paper. Hand stitch the machine-stitched line to the doll's head along the marked line. Repeat for the other side of the doll's head.

Pull the yarn to the back and twist it into a bun, braid it into one or two braids, or let it hang as a ponytail.

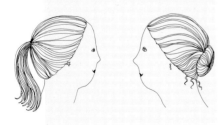

To dress up a hairstyle, make a separate braid and stitch or glue it to the doll's head. You can also combine two or more techniques.

To keep the hairstyle in place, sneak some glue onto the head under the yarn and press the yarn to the glue.

Flax, torn strips of fabric, ribbons, and many other materials can be crafted into doll hair using these same techniques.

Curling Yarn

Yarn is easy to curl. Wrap it around metal skewers or a metal knitting needle. Secure both ends with tape. Dampen the yarn with water or diluted

Stiffy™ fabric stiffener. Place in a 200°F (90°C) oven for fifteen minutes or until dry. Allow to cool. Slide the curls from the skewer.

These curls can be used to make a basic wig or can be added to many other hairstyles described here.

Denise Rominger, Cranbury, NJ

curly Crepe

Curly crepe is a soft wool fiber that is braided around a string. When the string is pulled, the braid comes apart into wavy lengths. Use curly crepe for any yarn hairstyle. It also works well when glued to the head with either a glue gun or white glue. It can be wound around the head and draped into ringlets.

"To make a curly hairdo for your doll, wrap yarn on a hairpin lace loom [available at yarn and needlework shops] set at a narrow width. Machine stitch down the center of the yarn. Pull the yarn from the loom. Twist it to form ringlets.

For hair try steel wool, narrow ribbon set into curls with a tiny curling iron, the mesh from onion bags, curling ribbon (the kind with messages is neat for a special occasion present), strung elbow macaroni to make curls, dried herbs, sequins, soutache, wood shavings, and mangled or eaten cassette tapes."

Beth Davison, Wilmington, DE

Fake fur

Fake fur makes a quick wig. Hold the fur over the head. Position it so the fur goes in the desired direction. Trim the fur's backing to fit inside the hairline. Cut just the backing, not the fur. Glue to the head. Comb the fur into the desired style, then mist with hair spray.

glued Yarn

For another no-sew hairstyle, glue yarn, curly crepe, perle cotton, or embroidery floss to the doll's head. The yarn can be in straight pieces, ringlets, or curls. First apply glue to the head and then simply lay the hair in place.

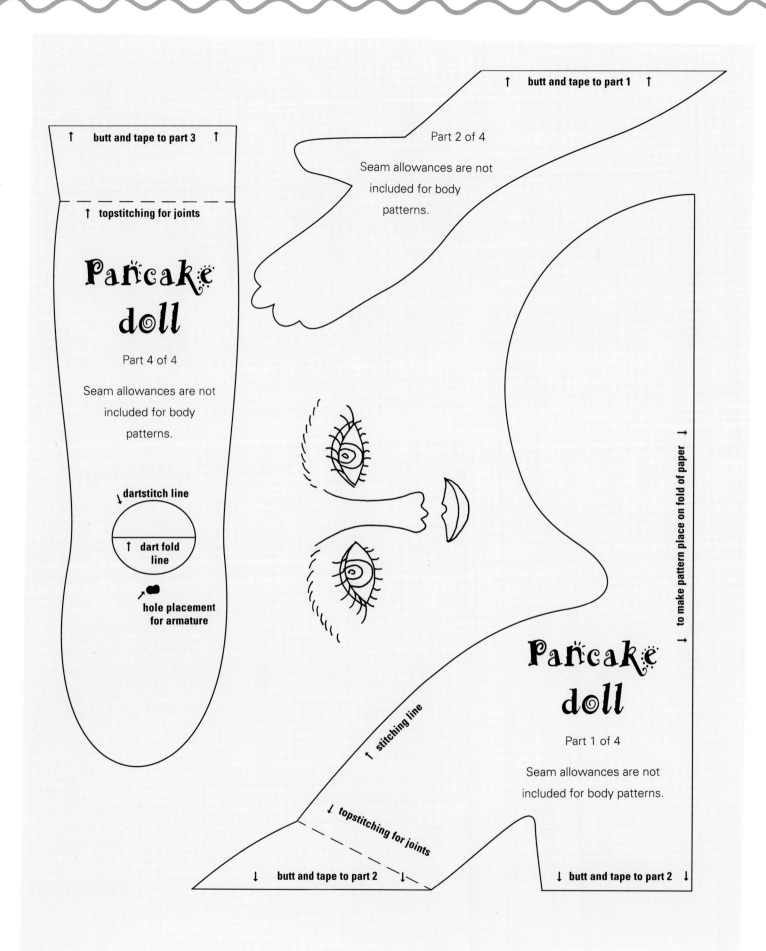

↑ butt and tape to part 3 ↑

↑ topstitching for joints

Pancake doll

Part 4 of 4

Seam allowances are not
included for body
patterns.

↓ dartstitch line

↑ dart fold
line

hole placement
for armature

↑ butt and tape to part 1 ↑

Part 2 of 4

Seam allowances are not
included for body
patterns.

→ to make pattern place on fold of paper →

↑ stitching line

Pancake doll

Part 1 of 4

Seam allowances are not
included for body patterns.

↓ topstitching for joints

↓ butt and tape to part 2 ↓

↓ butt and tape to part 2 ↓

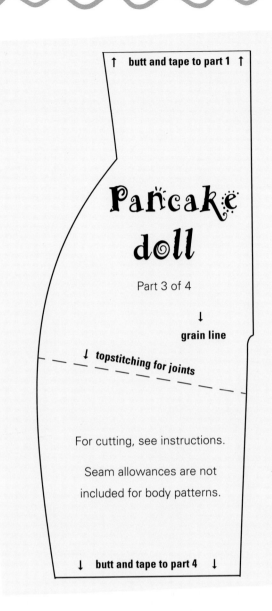

↑   butt and tape to part 1   ↑

Pancake doll

Part 3 of 4

↓

grain line

↓ **topstitching for joints**

For cutting, see instructions.

Seam allowances are not included for body patterns.

↓   butt and tape to part 4   ↓

Pancake doll

Bodice front

Cut 2 (1 is lining)

grain line ↑

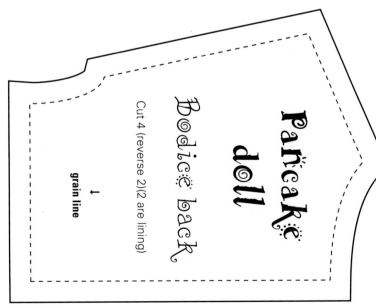

Pancake doll

Bodice back

Cut 4 (reverse 2)(2 are lining)

grain line ↑

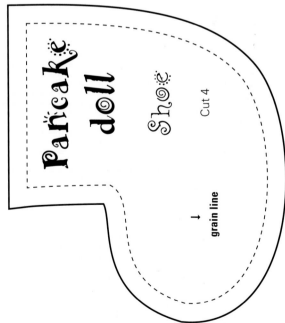

Pancake doll

Shoe

Cut 4

grain line ↑

chapter 4

Profile doll

The profile doll is a variation on the pancake doll, with separate arms and legs. Two arm and two leg choices are offered: choose pairs of matching limbs, or one from each pattern.

I've included patterns and written instructions for a dress, petticoat, cape, hat, and wings. With these you can make a witch, angel, or fairy if you wish. In addition, you can use the alternate body pattern to make a mermaid.

This doll is meant to be hung. She could also be supported from beneath with a "flying" doll stand.

Finished size: 13 to 14 inches (32.5 to 35cm) tall, depending upon which legs are used

Materials

Body
   ¼ yard (23cm) of fabric
   Matching thread
   Polyester fiberfill stuffing
Yarn for hair
Dental floss or carpet thread for thread jointing
Paint for shoes and face

Clothing

¼ yard (23cm) of fabric for dress
Matching thread
⅓ yard (30cm) of netting for petticoat
⅛ yard (11.5cm) of ¼-inch (6mm) -wide or smaller elastic for petticoat
¼ yard (23cm) of fabric for cape and hat
Matching thread
Small amount of fabric for wings
Small amount of batting for wings
Paint for the shoes and face

Instructions for Profile doll

1 Prepare the fabric and patterns as instructed on pages 12 and 13.

2 Lay the patterns on the fabric. Trace the outline, face, and other markings onto the fabric. Lay the marked fabric on another piece of body fabric, face markings down. Pin the layers together. (Doll instructions continue on page 50.)

Dyeing fabric

Fabrics in just the right "skin" shades are difficult to find. Many dollmakers resolve this problem by dyeing their own fabric.

Readily available in most grocery stores, Rit™ dye serves this purpose well. To achieve a believable Caucasian skin tone, I mix rose and peach in about a 1:2 ratio. For black skin, experiment with chocolate brown to get just the shade you desire. Likewise, try mixing beige, yellow, and light brown dye for Asian skin tones.

Start with a half yard to a yard (45 to 90cm) of fabric. Run it through the washing machine to remove any finishes. Cut a few swatches of the fabric for dye color tests.

Fill a sink with enough hot water to completely cover the fabric. Measure the dye and add it to the water. Stir. Dunk a fabric swatch into the dye bath and swish it around for a minute. Remove it. Rinse. Is it too rose or peach? Add more of the other color. Too light? Add more of both colors. Too dark? Dilute the dye solution with more hot water. Test again with another swatch.

Once the color is to your liking, submerge your wet fabric in the dye bath. Stir gently. Make sure you move the folds so you don't end up with streaky coloring.

When the color is slightly darker than you want it, drain the water from the sink. The color will lighten as the fabric dries. Rinse the fabric until no more dye comes out. Dry. Press while slightly damp.

Mermaid Variation

To appliqué the mermaid's tail, turn to page 17 and follow the instructions for appliquéd clothing. Use green velvet, lamé, or one of the glitzy fabrics in the special-occasion section of your fabric store. To make stitching much easier and to prevent fraying, apply fusible interfacing to the wrong side of lamé or any similar fabric before appliquéing.

Dress up the tail with rows of decorative stitching using colored

Bonnie Lewis, Herndon, VA

metallic thread. Add sequins and beads for even more aquatic shimmer. To construct the body and arms and to wig the doll, follow the instructions beginning on page 51.

Jodie Davis, Gainesville, VA

Turning body Parts

Using an arm as an example, here are instructions for turning small body parts. Assuming the opening is somewhere near the top of the arm, turn the top of the arm right side out. Unlock the jaws of a pair of hemostats. Insert the point into the arm. Push it all the way to the tip of the thumb. With your free hand, push the fabric at the tip of the thumb into the jaws of the hemostats. Clamp the jaws shut. Pull the

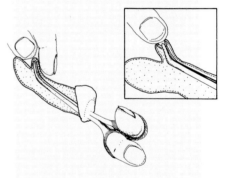

thumb into the hand. Unlock the hemostats.

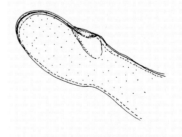

Insert the jaws of the hemostats into the hand. Clamp them onto the tips of the fingers. Pull the hemostats

3 (Continued from page 48.) Set your machine to a slightly shorter stitch length. Stitch just inside the traced lines. Backstitch at the beginning and ends of the stitching, stopping 1 inch (2.5cm) short of where you started, thus leaving an opening for turning.

4 Cut out the doll pieces, leaving a ⅛-inch (3mm) seam allowance, except at the openings, where it should be about ¼ inch (6mm). Clip into concave curves. Apply Fray Check to the raw edges at the openings and to the clips.

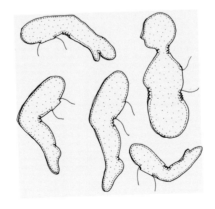

5 Turn the pieces right side out. (Doll instructions continue on page 51.)

out of the arm gently. Work the arm right side out, much like you would a pantyhose leg, pulling the fingertips out of the opening at the top of the arm.

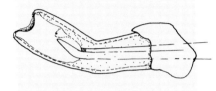

Insert the Stuff-It™, or other pointed tool, into the arm. Run the tip all around the seam allowance to push the arm out fully to smooth the seams.

> "If the arms or legs are a bit lumpy after stuffing I put the part that needs smoothing between my palms and roll it as if working with clay or making a bread-stick. That is often all it takes to smooth out the lumps. This works best with good quality stuffing."
>
> Madeline Molis,
> Rancho Palos Verdes, CA

6 (Continued from page 50.) Stuff the body parts. (See page 20 for more information on how to stuff a doll.)

7 Ladderstitch (see page 21) the openings of the body parts closed.

Clothing and jointing

dress

1 For the dress, cut one 7½- by 12-inch (18.5 by 30cm) rectangle. For the petticoat, cut one 10- by 18-inch (25 by 45cm) rectangle. For the cape, cut one 8- by 10-inch (20 by 25cm) rectangle. For the lower sleeves, cut two 2¾- by 3½-inch (7 by 9cm) rectangles.

2 Fold the dress rectangle so that the matching short edges and the right sides are together. Stitch the short edges together. Press the seam open.

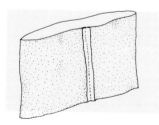

3 On one raw edge, press ¼ inch (6mm) to the wrong side. Repeat for

the other raw edge. Gather along one edge. (This will be the neck opening.) Put the dress on the doll. Pull up the gathering to fit the doll. Tie the threads together.

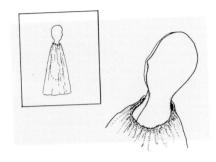

4 Stitch two upper-sleeve pieces together, right sides facing. Repeat for the two remaining upper-sleeve pieces. Gather the raw edges at the lower edges of the upper sleeves. Turn right side out. Press. Put the upper sleeves on the arms.

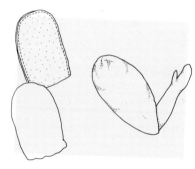

5 Thread a dollmaking needle with doubled carpet thread or a single strand of dental floss and knot the thread. Push the needle into the body side of one leg at the dot. Come out on the outside of the leg. Go in through the same hole. By using the same hole at the outside of the leg, the thread will go into the leg and nestle in the stuffing. This avoids a pulled pucker on the visible side of the doll's arm or leg. Come out on the inside of the leg again, but not in the same hole.

6 Push the needle into the appropriate body side at the dot and emerge out of the other side of the body. Attach the second leg as you did the first. Go back through the body. Pull tightly. Knot the thread between the body and the leg.

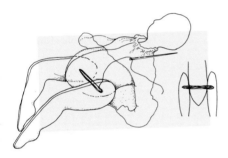

7 Joint the arms as you did the legs, pulling up the sleeve so you can reach the top of the arm. Thread through the arm, inside the upper sleeves, dress, and body, into the second arm, and inside the upper sleeve on the opposite side.

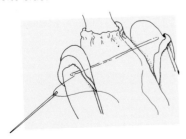

8 Pull up on the gathering stitches at the lower edge of the upper sleeves. Tie the ends in knots.

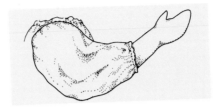

9 Fold the lower sleeves in half, wrong sides together, so that the short edges match. Fold the matched raw edges ¼ inch (6mm) to one side. Place the lower sleeve on the doll as shown, overlapping the folded edge of the lower sleeve over the gathered edge of the upper sleeve. Turn one raw edge of the lower sleeve to the wrong side, overlapping the other long edge. Hand stitch this overlap. Hand stitch the top edge over the sleeve.

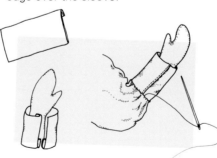

10 Right sides together, fold the petticoat so that the shorter edges match. Stitch. Fold the petticoat so the longer

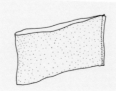

edges match, wrong sides together. Stitch a bit more than ¼ inch (6mm) from the folded edge, leaving a ½-inch (12mm) opening.

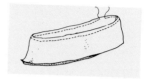

11 Insert a piece of elastic through the opening. Put the petticoat on the doll. Adjust the elastic to fit. Pin. Remove the petticoat from the doll. Trim the elastic ends, overlap, and stitch them together.

12 Press ¼ inch (6mm) on one raw edge of the cape to the wrong side. Repeat for the remaining three sides. Topstitch. Gather one edge of the cape.

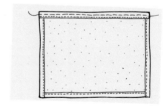

13 Right sides together, stitch the two collar pieces together. Leave a ½-inch (12mm) -long opening at the center of the shorter of the long edges.

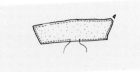

Trim the seam allowance. Turn right side out. Press. Pull up on the cape's gathering stitches to fit the short side of the collar. Hand stitch the collar to

the cape. Hand stitch the front top edges of the cape to the doll.

14 Apply the face using one of the methods described on pages 107 to 111. Paint the shoes from the marked line down.

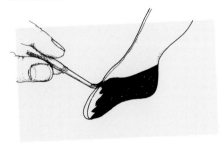

Jodie Davis, Gainesville, VA

Hair

〰〰〰〰〰〰

1 To make hair for the doll, loop the yarn as shown. The amount of yarn used depends upon the thickness of the yarn. The length is up to you. Use as much as you think you need. You can easily add more later.

53

2 Draw a 1½-inch (4cm) -long line on a piece of paper. Place the center of the yarn across the line. Machine stitch the yarn to the paper.

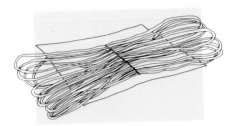

3 Tear the paper from the yarn. Try the wig on the doll. If you need to add more yarn, lay the wig on another piece of paper and stitch more yarn right on top of the previous stitching. Once you have sufficient yarn, place the wig on the doll so that the stitching forms a "part." Hand stitch over the machine stitching to secure the wig to the head.

4 For feather hair, use long, skinny feathers. Glue them around the sides and back of the head and trim the quills as necessary. The quills will be covered by the hat.

For more ideas on wigging your doll, see pages 39 to 43.

Hat

~~~~~~~~~~

1 Right sides together, stitch the straight edges of one hat-top piece together. Trim the seam allowance. Repeat for the second hat-top piece.

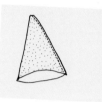

2 Turn one hat top right side out. Put inside the second hat top. Stitch the raw edges together. Trim the seam allowance to ⅛ inch (3mm).

3 Make a slash in one hat top about ½ inch (12mm) wide. Turn the hat right side out through this slash. The slash will be inside the hat and therefore hidden.

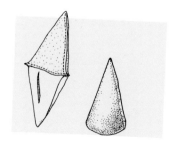

4 Right sides together, stitch the two hat brim pieces together. Slash through both pieces as shown.

5 Turn right side out. Put the hat brim on the doll over her wig. Put the hat top on top. Stitch the hat top to the head through the hat brim.

Wings

~~~~~~~~~~

1 Right sides together, lay the wing fabrics on top of the batting. Stitch all the way around the wings. Trim the seam allowance, including the batting, to ⅛ inch (3mm). Slash the wings at the center as shown.

Jodie Davis, Gainesville, VA

Depending upon the size and shape of the doily, you can leave it as is or stitch a row of basting stitches along the center to gather it to match the length of the doll's back.

"To stiffen and shape the doily wings, bend a sheet of aluminum foil into a 'V' to form a drying rack. Saturate the wings with Stiffy™ fabric stiffener or white glue mixed with water to the consistency of heavy cream. Drape the wings on the foil form so the center line of the wings, which will be stitched to the doll's back, is along the top fold in the foil. Allow to dry."

Donna Murray,
South St. Paul, MN

2 Turn wings right side out. Press. Machine embroider, quilt, or otherwise adorn the wings. Stitch to the doll's back.

Options: Instead of using batting, try crinoline or craft bond. These will give your doll a thinner, stiffer wing.

For a lacy effect, choose a doily or a pair of lace collars for the wings.

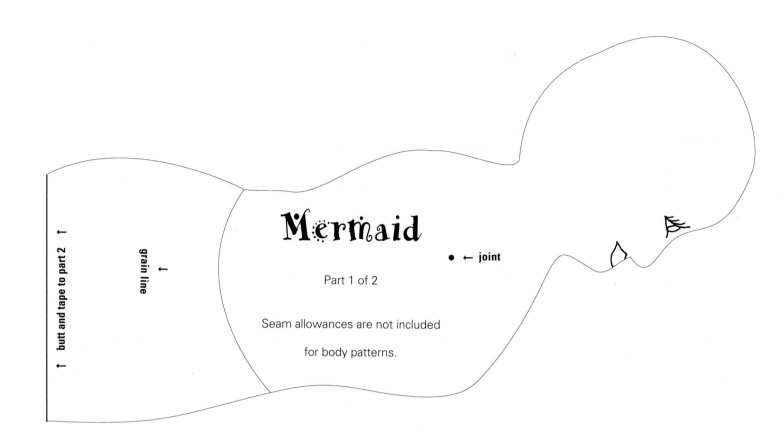

Mermaid

← joint

Part 1 of 2

Seam allowances are not included

for body patterns.

↑ butt and tape to part 2 ↑

grain line ↑

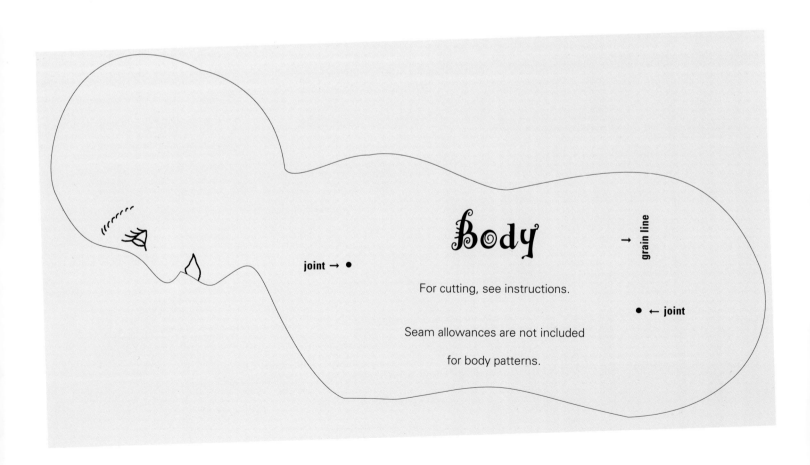

Body

joint → ●

↑ grain line

For cutting, see instructions.

● ← joint

Seam allowances are not included

for body patterns.

Mermaid

Part 2 of 2

For cutting, see instructions.

Seam allowances are not included for body patterns.

→ butt and tape to part 1 →

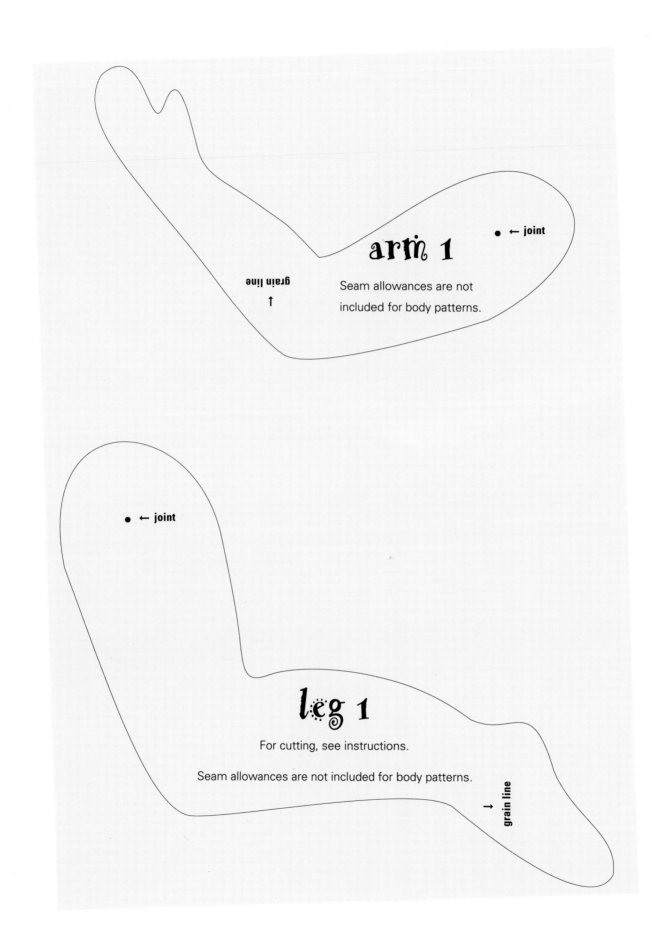

arm 1

← joint

grain line

Seam allowances are not
included for body patterns.

← joint

leg 1

For cutting, see instructions.

Seam allowances are not included for body patterns.

grain line

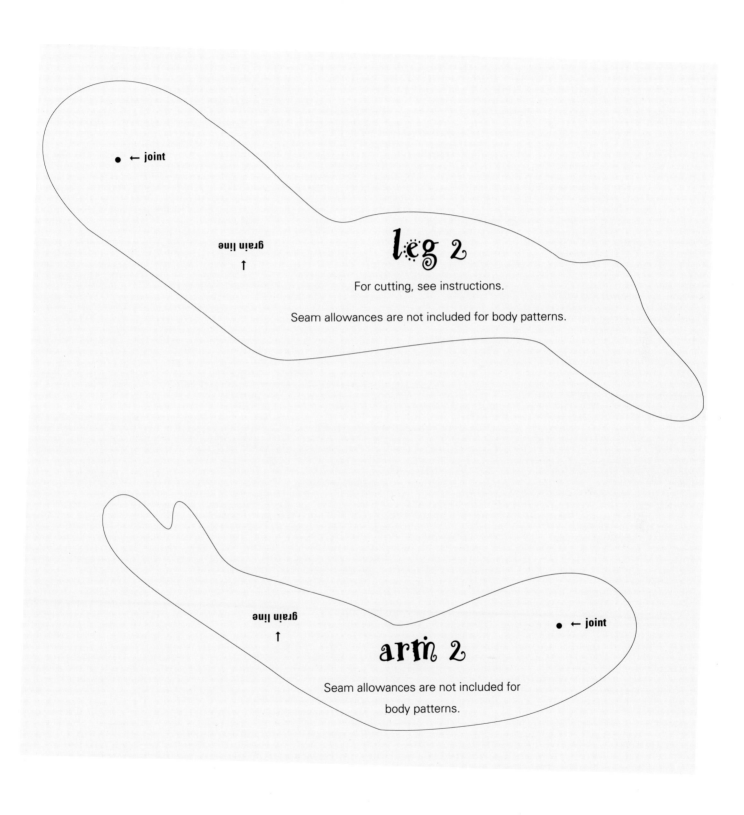

● ← joint

↑ grain line

leg 2

For cutting, see instructions.

Seam allowances are not included for body patterns.

↑ grain line

arm 2

● ← joint

Seam allowances are not included for
body patterns.

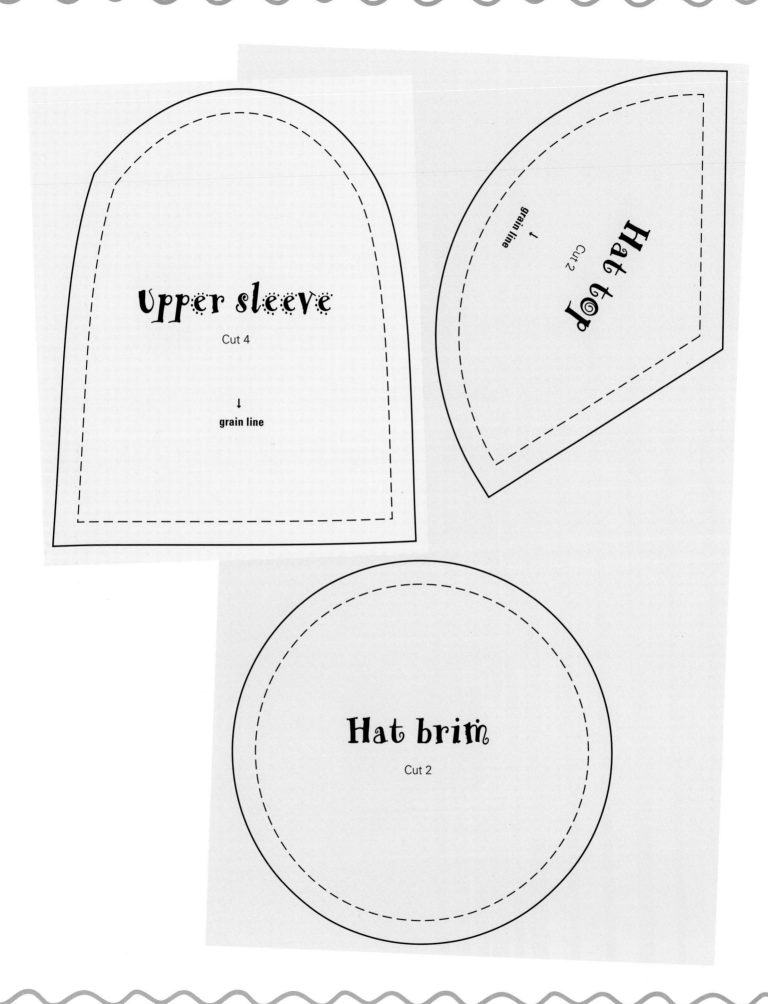

Upper sleeve

Cut 4

↓

grain line

Hat top

Cut 2

↑

grain line

Hat brim

Cut 2

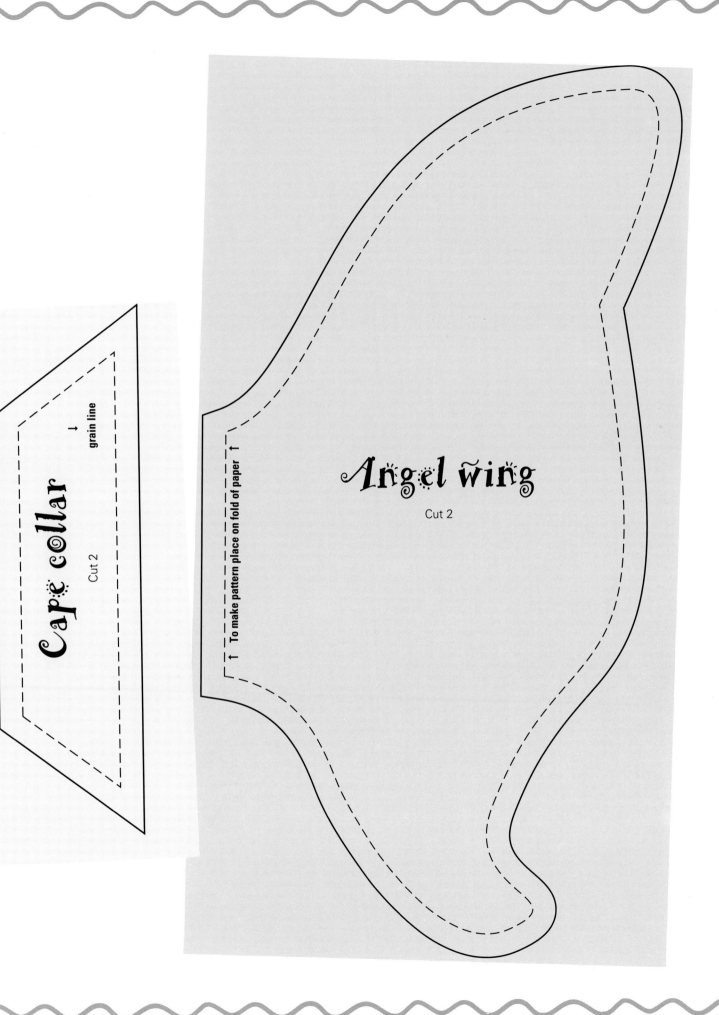

Cape collar

Cut 2

→ grain line

Angel wing

Cut 2

← To make pattern place on fold of paper ↑

chapter 5

Baby

doll

You can make a baby, a toddler, or a cherub with this pattern. Use flannel or fleece fabric to make a soft, cuddly baby. I've included a pattern for a zippered sleeper, but you may dress your baby in purchased clothing.

For the toddler dolls, use the longer arm and leg patterns. You will find instructions for toddler boy and girl outfits including two doll sweaters made from one old adult sweater. Purchased doll or baby shoes measuring $3\frac{1}{2}$ to 4 inches (9 to 10cm) will fit the dolls.

For a third option I have reduced the pattern to make a little cherub—a perfect Christmas tree ornament or decoration for a Valentine's Day gift.

In this chapter you will also learn how to install doll joints, making these dolls truly lifelike.

An important point to remember for this or any doll: If you attach buttons, beads, or charms to your doll it is not suitable for children under three years of age.

Finished sizes: Baby Doll, 19 inches (47.5cm) tall; Toddlers, 22 inches (55cm) tall; Cherub, $5\frac{1}{2}$ inches (14cm) tall

Materials

Body for Baby or Toddler

$\frac{1}{2}$ yard (45cm) of muslin

Matching thread

Polyester fiberfill stuffing

Four sets of $1\frac{1}{2}$-inch (4cm) plastic doll joints

Plastic pellets (optional) (see Sources, page 124)

Baby doll

$\frac{5}{8}$ yard (57cm) of flannel

Matching thread

7-inch (17cm) zipper

2- by $11\frac{1}{2}$-inch (5 by 29cm) bias strip

$\frac{1}{3}$ yard (30cm) of $1\frac{1}{2}$-inch (4cm) -wide eyelet

$\frac{5}{8}$ yard (57cm) of $\frac{1}{4}$-inch (4cm) -wide elastic

Doll wig (Sugar in Auburn)

Paint or embroidery floss for face

Toddler girl

Two $\frac{1}{2}$-inch (12mm) black half round shank buttons

Black or brown and red embroidery floss

Two skeins of yarn (I used $\frac{1}{8}$ pound [56.5g] of Natural Copper Wave, from Fleece and Unicorn; see Sources, page 124)

Matching thread

Discarded sweater

Matching thread

Lace collar

11- by 30-inch (27.5 by 75cm) piece of corduroy

Matching thread

14 inches (35cm) of $\frac{1}{4}$-inch (6mm) -wide elastic

3- by 18-inch (7 by 45cm) piece of fabric or ribbon for sash

Three small buttons for sweater

Baby or doll shoes and stockings

$\frac{3}{4}$ yard (68cm) of 1-inch (2.5cm) -wide ribbon for hair bow

Embroidery floss for face

Two $\frac{3}{8}$-inch (9mm) round domed black buttons for eyes

Toddler boy

Two $\frac{1}{2}$-inch (12mm) black half round shank buttons

Black or brown and red embroidery floss

Two skeins of yarn (I used $\frac{1}{8}$ pound [56.5g] of Natural Copper Wave, from Fleece and Unicorn; see Sources, page 124)

Matching thread

Discarded sweater

Matching thread

$\frac{1}{2}$ yard (45cm) of corduroy

Matching thread

$\frac{5}{8}$ yard (57cm) of $\frac{1}{4}$-inch (6mm) -wide elastic

Baby or doll shoes and socks

5- by 14-inch (12.5 by 35cm) piece of fabric for bow tie

2- by 11-inch (5 by 27.5cm) piece of rib knit for mock turtleneck

$\frac{1}{4}$ yard (23cm) of fabric for hat

Embroidery floss for face

Two $\frac{3}{8}$-inch (9mm) round domed black buttons for eyes

Cherub

Scrap of muslin

Matching thread

Polyester fiberfill stuffing

Scraps of yarn

Metallic paper or Battenburg lace doily for wings

Heart charm

Scrap of ribbon

Paint for face

Fabrics

Good quality muslin is the standard fabric of choice for cloth dolls. It can be used as is, tea-dyed for an antique look, or dyed to a more skinlike shade.

But don't stop there. I make baby dolls from flannel and pajama fleece. The warm, cuddly feel of the fabric is perfect for a huggable baby doll. Hand-dyed and marbled fabrics are making a quick migration to doll-making from their fast growing popularity in quiltmaking. Truly adventurous dollmakers use any fabric imaginable: velvet, solid fabrics of any color, small and large print fabrics—any fabric that speaks "doll" to them.

Diane Roode Schneck, New York, NY

Marcia Spencer of Delevan, New York, prefers cotton knit, which she tea-dyes to just the right shade.

Sandy Wheeler of Morrison, Colorado, seldom uses muslin. "I really like the 'difficult' fabrics and frequently use satin, taffeta, and other fun fabrics for doll bodies. I usually back these fabrics with lightweight iron-on inter-facing. And I double stitch small details like fingers."

Instructions for Baby doll and Toddler

1 Prepare the patterns and fabric as instructed on pages 12 and 13.

2 Cut two body sides/backs and one body front from the muslin. Transfer face markings to the right side of the body front.

3 Stitch the two body side/back pieces together along the center back, right sides together. Leave a 3-inch (7cm) -long opening between the dots for turning and stuffing. Right sides together, match one side of the body front to the appropriate body side/back. Repeat for the other side. Trim seam allowances to ⅛ inch (3mm).

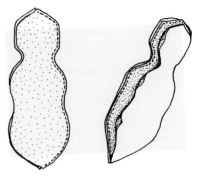

4 For the arms and legs, fold the fabric and lay the pattern pieces on top, leaving a minimum of ½ inch (12mm) between them. Trace around the patterns on the stitching line. Trace the dart and joint markings. (I make holes at the joint markings so I can put a dot right through the paper into the fabric, and I cut the darts out of the pattern so I can trace them along the cut edges.) Stitch just inside all the traced lines, leaving the darts and the toes unstitched. Leave an opening between the dots on each leg and arm for turning and stuffing as indicated on the patterns.

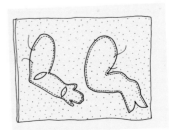

5 Cut the pieces out, leaving a ⅛-inch (3mm) seam allowance, ¼-inch (6mm) at the openings.

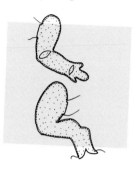

6 Fold the legs so that the seams match. Stitch ¼ inch (6mm) from the raw edge at the toes. Trim seam allowance to ⅛ inch (3mm).

7 Crease the arm darts. Stitch along the marked lines, making sure to catch the fabric of one arm piece only. Make darts on the inside arms only. This will allow the baby's arms to bend around her body.

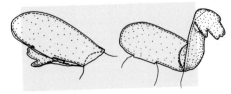

8 Make holes for joints at markings on inside legs and arms. To make sure that you make a right and a left leg,

hold them together and make the holes on the sides of the legs that face one another. Make holes in the body at the markings for the arms and legs. Apply Fray Check™ to all holes and clips. Allow to dry.

Turn all body parts right side out.

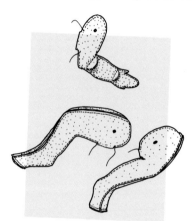

"For added strength at the joint locations when using lightweight fabrics, apply fusible web to a scrap of fabric measuring roughly 6 inches [15cm] square. Cut the fabric into circles measuring about ¾-inch [2cm] wide. Fuse the fabric to the wrong sides of the arms, legs, and body over the joint holes. Make holes through the fabric circles. This will act as a reinforcement."

Patti Welsh,
North Ft. Meyers, FL

9 Insert the piece of the joint that has the post on it into an arm or leg. Poke the post out of the hole. Repeat for all arms and legs.

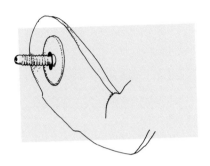

10 Push the post protruding from one arm into the appropriate hole in the body. Double-check to be sure you are putting the correct arm on the proper side. Put a large plastic washer onto the post inside the body. Put the small locking washer onto the post inside the body. Push to snap it down as far as it will go. Repeat for the remaining limbs.

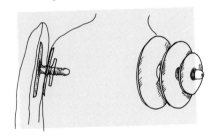

11 Stuff the arms and legs. (See page 20 for instructions on stuffing your doll with fiberfill, or page 67 for instructions on stuffing your doll with plastic pellets.) (Doll instructions continue on page 67.)

"I signed my doll by drawing a heart on the doll's chest. I then signed my name and the date. I did this on a doll I made for my daughter Mary's birthday. She constantly reads the signature and the birthday wishes I wrote on the doll."

Roni Gerhardt,
Danbury, CT

Stuffing with plastic pellets

For added realism, stuff your baby doll with plastic pellets. Cradled in your arms, she will have a lifelike feel and she will even sit by herself. Though dried peas and sand are also commonly used, plastic pellets are clean and do not attract pests.

When stitching your doll, leave an opening for turning at the top of the doll's head. You can then scoop the pellets into a funnel and fill the body from bottom to top.

As you fill the body with pellets, lift the doll to straighten any folds in the fabric. Stir the pellets occasionally to fill any air spaces.

1 Stuff the toes of one leg with fiberfill. Pour pellets into the leg to fill the center of the foot. Stuff the heel with fiberfill. Continue filling the lower legs with pellets up to the knee. Stuff the front of the knee with fiberfill. Fill the upper leg with pellets. Stuff the top of the leg with fiberfill. Repeat for the second leg.

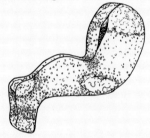

2 Stuff the fingers and hand up to the dart with fiberfill, then fill the forearm with pellets. Continue stuffing the elbow with fiberfill. Stuff the upper arm with pellets. Finally, finish the arm by stuffing the top with fiberfill.

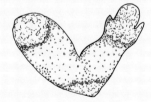

3 Line the bottom of the doll with fiberfill to give it shape. Fill the doll's body up to the bottom of the neck with pellets.

4 Stuff the neck and line the face with fiberfill, then fill the head with pellets. Stuff to the opening with fiberfill.

5 Whipstitch (see page 21) the opening at the top of the head closed.

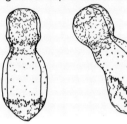

12 (Continued from page 66.) Ladderstitch (see page 21) all seam openings closed.

13 Fold a piece of the fabric with right sides together. Trace the ear pattern onto the fabric. Flip and trace again. Stitch just inside the marked lines, overlapping the stitching ¼ inch (6mm) or so. Trim the seam allowance to ⅛ inch (3mm) or less. To make a right and a left ear, hold them together and make slashes on the sides that touch. Turn the ears right side out. Draw the curve onto the unslashed side of each ear. Topstitch along the marking. With the slashed sides against the head, slipstitch the ears to the doll.

Needle Sculpting

To needle-sculpt the fingers and toes, make tiny backstitches as shown. Begin and end by inserting the needle into the fabric and emerging where you wish to begin your stitching. Pull on the thread to pop the knot into the stuffing inside the doll, just as you would when quilting.

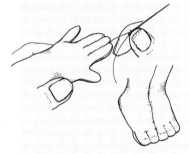

To indent the eyes, thread a long dollmaking needle with quilting thread. Knot the end. Go into the back of the head where the knot will be covered by the hair. Emerge at one corner of an eye on the eye outline. Go back in just a thread or two away along the eye outline. Emerge from the back of the head. Pull on the thread to indent the eye. Knot the thread. Repeat for the other side of the eye. Repeat for the other eye. To make a belly button for your doll, cover a button-to-cover with body fabric. Stitch to the appropriate spot on the doll.

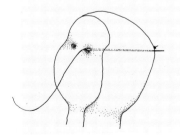

Cherub

1 Make the cherub by following the instructions for the baby doll, with these changes: use a ⅛-inch (3mm) allowance and joint the cherub using the thread-jointing method on page 32.

2 To finish the cherub, paint its face and add wings, hair, and embellishments.

3 If you are using a doily for the wings, fold the doily in half. Stitch or glue to cherub's back.

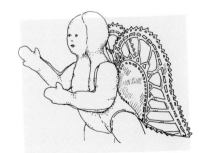

4 For a tousled hairstyle, mix up yarn in a flattened ball, then glue to the cherub's head.

5 Drape and tie or glue ribbons around the cherub's neck and chest.

6 Glue or stitch the charm in the cherub's hands or to the ribbon.

Baby doll hair

For a yarn wig, turn to the hair-making section on pages 39 to 43.

If using a purchased wig, position the wig on the head and glue into place.

Jodie Davis, Gainesville, VA

Baby doll sleeper

Jodie Davis, Gainesville, VA

1 Right sides together, baste the two front pieces together along the center front from the neck edge to the dot. At the dot, switch to a regular length stitch, backstitch, and continue stitching down to the crotch. Press the seam open.

2 Lay the sleeper front right side down. Apply glue stick to the right side of the zipper tape. Lay the zipper right side down on the seam allowance of the sleeper, having the top of the zipper ½ inch (6mm) below the neck edge of the sleeper. Match the center of the zipper teeth with the basting. Press to

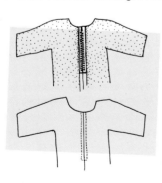

glue the zipper in place. Topstitch the zipper to the sleeper along the stitching line marked on the zipper tape.

3 Right sides together, stitch the sleeper front to the back at shoulder seams, then press the seams open.

4 Press 1½ inches (4cm) at the lower edge of each sleeve to the wrong side. Cut two pieces of elastic, each 4 inches (10cm) long. Zigzag one piece of elastic to one sleeve, covering the raw edge and stretching the elastic to fit as you sew. This will form a ruffle. Repeat for the second sleeve.

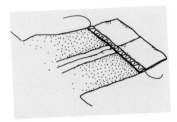

5 Stitch the side and sleeve seams as one .

6 The legs of the sleeper are treated much as the sleeves. Press 1½ inches (4cm) to the wrong side at the lower edge of each leg. Cut two 6-inch (15cm) -long pieces of elastic and zigzag them to the leg edges, with one edge of the elastic along the raw edge of the doubled fabric, stretching the elastic to fit as you sew.

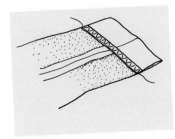

7 Stitch the crotch seam.

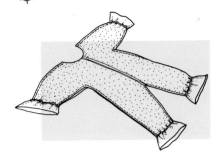

8 Gather stitch the neck edge just inside the ¼-inch (6mm) seam allowance. Pin each end of the neck binding to the ends of the wrong side of the neck edge, having the binding extend ½ inch (12mm) past the raw edge. Pull up on the gathering stitches to fit the binding. Pin and baste the binding to the neck.

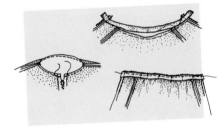

9 Baste the lace to the right side of the neck edge, having the wrong side of the lace facing the right side of the sleeper. Trim the ends of the lace ½ inch (12mm) past the front edges of the sleeper, then turn them under to align with the edges of the sleeper.

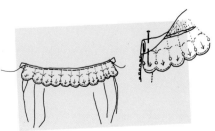

10 Fold the long raw edge of the binding under ¼ inch (6mm). Fold the binding over the lace. Turn the short raw ends of the binding under. From the right side, topstitch close to the bottom fold, securing the lace and the binding.

toddlers' faces

1 Thread an embroidery needle with brown or black embroidery floss. Knot one end. Go into the center of one eye marking so that the knot will be hidden under the eye. Embroider eyebrows and lashes. End by emerging from the center of the eye and knot.

2 Likewise, start and end the mouth in the center of the eye, using the same technique as described in step 1. Leave the floss loose enough to follow the shape of the mouth. Use a tiny drop of glue to hold the floss in a smile.

3 For the eyes, using a long doll-making needle and strong thread or waxed dental floss, push the needle into the back of the head and emerge from the center of one eye.

4 Put the eye shank onto the needle and thread. Go back in at the center of the eye and come out at the back of the head. Pull on the floss tightly, causing the eye to dent into the fabric. Make a knot. Repeat for the second eye.

Boy's hair

1 Cut the yarn into 10- to 12-inch (25 to 30cm) lengths. Group them and tie the center of the bunch together with one of the pieces.

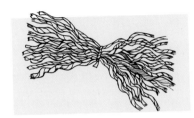

2 Unwind the twists in the yarn. The easiest way to do this is to grasp two of the four strands in each hand and pull. Let the wig twirl freely, thereby unwinding the yarn.

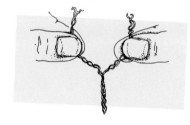

3 Hand stitch the yarn to the center top of the head about ¾ inch (2cm) behind the junction of the seams at the top of the head.

4 Arrange the yarn evenly around the head. Lift up one section of the hair at a time, then apply glue to the head. Press the yarn back in place and trim the bangs above the eyebrows. Trim the hair around the head.

girl's hair

1 The girl's hair is made in three sections. For the center section cut ten pieces of yarn, each 14 inches (35cm) long. Draw a 2-inch (5cm) -long line on a piece of paper. Lay the yarn across the line, having 2 inches extend to one side of the line. This will be the bangs. Machine stitch along the line several times. Tear the paper away from each side of the stitching.

2 Cut the remaining yarn into 29-inch (72.5cm) lengths. This will form the hair for the sides of the head. Divide and make two sections of hair as follows: draw a 2½-inch (6.5cm) -long line on a piece of paper. Lay half of the yarn pieces across the line, with the center of the yarn along the line. Stitch along the line over the yarn several times. Tear the paper from the stitch-

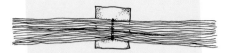

ing. Repeat this procedure for the last of the yarn.

3 To unwind the twists in the yarn, grasp two of the four strands in each hand and pull. Let the hair twirl, thereby unwinding the yarn. Repeat for all of the yarn in each of the hair sections.

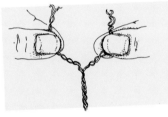

4 Straighten one of the two identical hair side sections so that it is smooth and lays flat as stitched, with yarn to each side of the stitching. Lay the stitching in a vertical line just behind the head side seam with the lower edge even with the bottom of the eye. Hand stitch along the part from the bottom to the top. Repeat with the

Jodie Davis, Gainesville, VA

second hair section on the other side of the head.

5 Lay the center hair section along the center top of the head so the stitching is between and in line with that of the hair sections you just hand stitched. Hand stitch along the machine stitching to secure the yarn to the head.

6 Pull the hair at the sides of the head to the back. Tie the ribbon around the hair and into a bow at the top of the head.

Sweaters

Two doll sweaters can be made from one adult sweater.

1 Lay the sweater out smoothly. For the girl's sweater, lay the sweater pattern on the sweater, with the lower edge of the pattern even with that of the sweater; pin. Cut out the sweater.

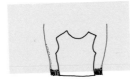

For the boy's sweater, match the ribbing at the front and back of the top of the sweater. Lay the pattern on the sweater; pin. Cut out the sweater.

2 For the girl's sweater, cut the sleeves off at about a thirty-degree angle at the top of the sweater sleeve. Cut the bottom of the sleeve about 6 inches (15cm) below the first cut.

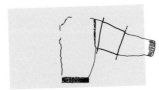

For the boy's sweater sleeves, cut off the bottoms of the sleeves so they are about 7 inches (17cm) long. Re-stitch the existing underarm sleeve seam so it is 6 inches long. Turn wrong side out.

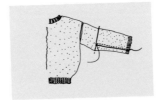

3 Stitch the shoulder and side seams of either sweater.

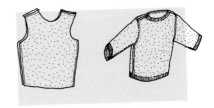

4 Gather the shoulder edge of the girl's sleeves to fit the armhole. Pin and stitch the sleeves to the armholes.

5 For the girl, turn ¼ inch (6mm) to the wrong side at the neck opening. Hand stitch. Put the sweater on the doll. Stitch the lace collar over the neckline.

For the boy's dickey, stitch the short edges of the ribbing together. Fold in half with the wrong sides together. Put the dickey on the doll, hiding the raw edge under the neckline of the sweater. Tuck the lower edge of the sweater into the boy's pants.

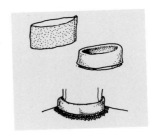

6 For the girl's sleeves, turn ¼ inch (6mm) under on the lower edge of the sleeve. Using long stitches, hand baste the lower edge. Put the sweater on the

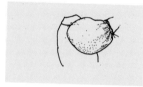

doll. Pull up on the thread. Tie a knot. Cut a piece of lace 6 inches (15cm) long. Right sides together, stitch the short ends together. Put the lace on

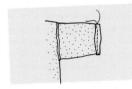

the doll's arm, just under the lower edge of the sleeve. Stitch to the bottom edge of the sleeve.

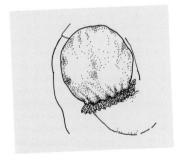

skirt

1 For the hem, press one long raw edge of the skirt ¼ inch (6mm) to the wrong side. With the right side of the

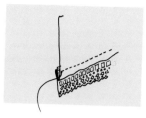

lace facing the wrong side of the skirt, topstitch the lace to the hem of the skirt.

2 Right sides together, stitch the two short ends of the skirt together.

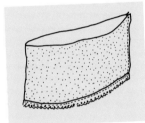

3 Press ¼ inch (6mm), then ½ inch (12mm) to the wrong side along the remaining raw edge. Topstitch close to the bottom fold, leaving a ½-inch opening to insert the elastic.

4 Cut a piece of elastic 14 inches (35cm) long. Put safety pins on both ends. Insert one safety pin into the casing and pull through, emerging where you began. Overlap the ends and stitch. Topstitch the opening closed.

Sash

1 Wrong sides together, seam the two long edges of the sash. Press the sash in half with the seam at center (this will be the back).

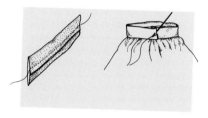

2 Wrap the sash snugly around the doll's waist. Overlap the ends at the back. Turn the raw end of the sash that is on top to the wrong side. Hand stitch sash in place.

knickers

1 Fold one knicker piece in half so the wrong sides are facing. Stitch the inside leg seam. Repeat for the second knicker piece.

Jodie Davis, Gainesville, VA

2 Turn one knicker piece right side out and slip it inside the other. Match the raw edges of the crotch seam. Pin. Stitch. Turn the knickers right side out.

3 At waist edge, press ¼ inch (6mm), then ½ inch (12mm) to the wrong side. Topstitch close to the fold, leaving a ½-inch-long opening.

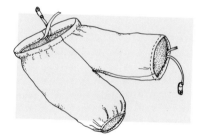

4 Cut a piece of elastic 14 inches (35cm) long. Attach a safety pin to each end. Insert one safety pin into the casing and pull through, emerging where you began. Overlap the ends and stitch. Topstitch the opening closed.

5 For each leg hem, press ¼ inch (6mm), then ½ inch to the wrong side. Topstitch close to the fold, leaving a ½-inch-long opening.

6 Cut a piece of elastic 4 inches (10cm) long. Attach a safety pin to each end. Insert one safety pin into the casing and push all the way through, emerging where you began. Overlap the ends and stitch. Topstitch the opening closed. Repeat for the other leg.

Tie

1 Right sides together, seam the long raw edges of the tie. Turn right side out. Press so the seam is at the center. Cut off 3 inches (7cm) for the tie center. Fold the tie so the ends overlap about 1 inch (2.5 cm).

2 Wrap the tie center around the center of the tie. Fold the raw edges of the tie center to the back. Whipstitch (see page 21).

3 Stitch tie to the sweater front.

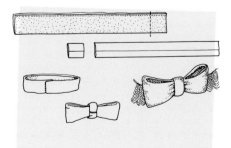

hat

1 For both the hat and the hat lining, stitch the hat top to the hat bottom along the large circular outside edges, right sides together.

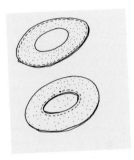

2 Trim the seam allowance to ⅛ inch (3mm). Turn one hat right side out. Press both hat and lining.

3 Put one hat piece inside the second hat so the right sides are together. Stitch the raw circular edges together, leaving a 3-inch (7cm) -long opening for turning.

4 Turn the hat right side out. Stitch the opening closed.

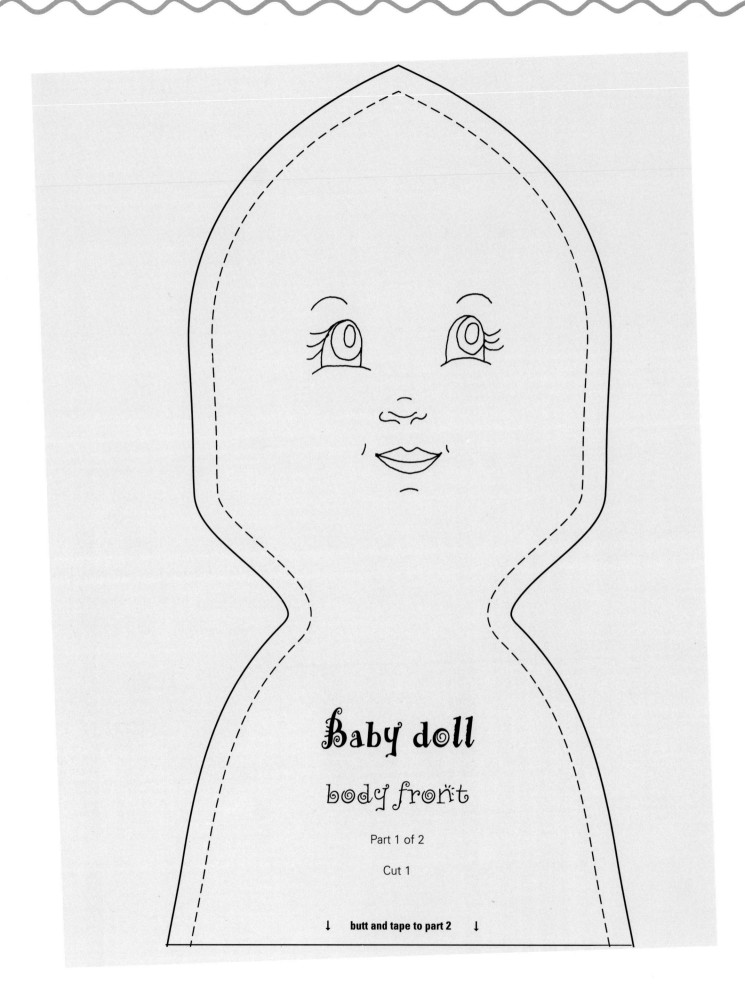

Baby doll

body front

Part 1 of 2

Cut 1

↓   **butt and tape to part 2**   ↓

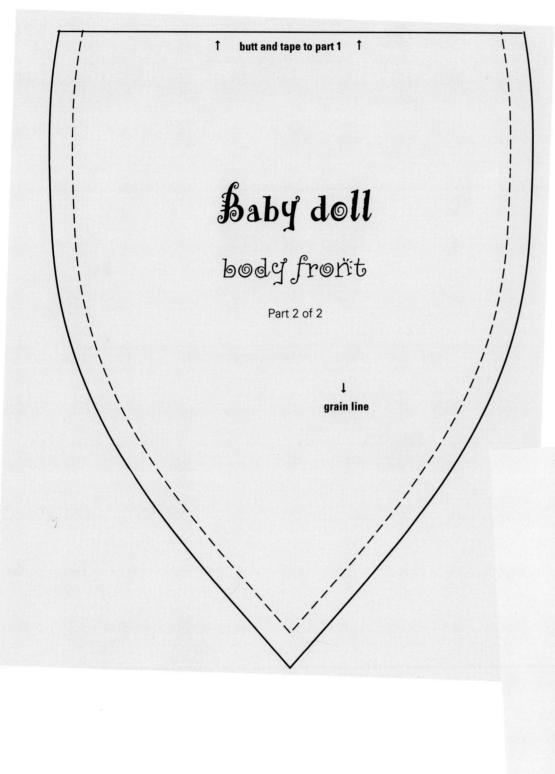

↑   **butt and tape to part 1**   ↑

Baby doll

body front

Part 2 of 2

↓

grain line

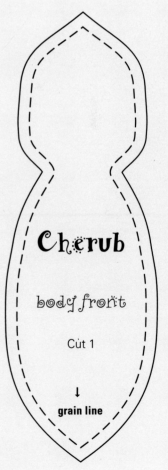

Cherub

body front

Cut 1

↓

grain line

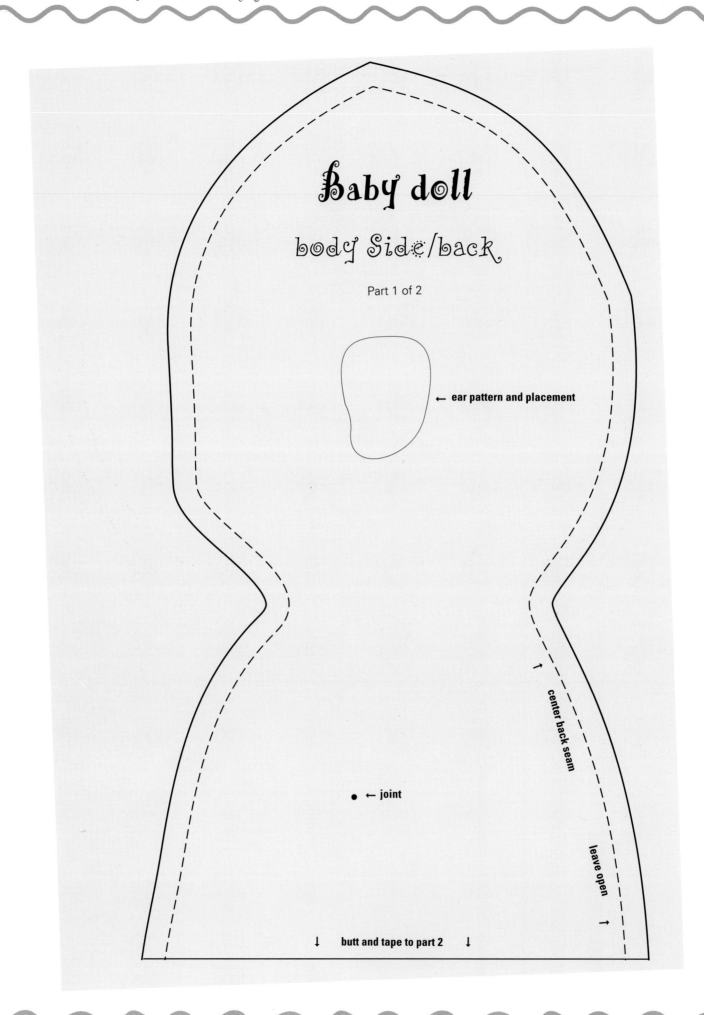

Baby doll

body side/back

Part 1 of 2

← ear pattern and placement

• ← joint

center back seam

leave open

↓　　butt and tape to part 2　　↓

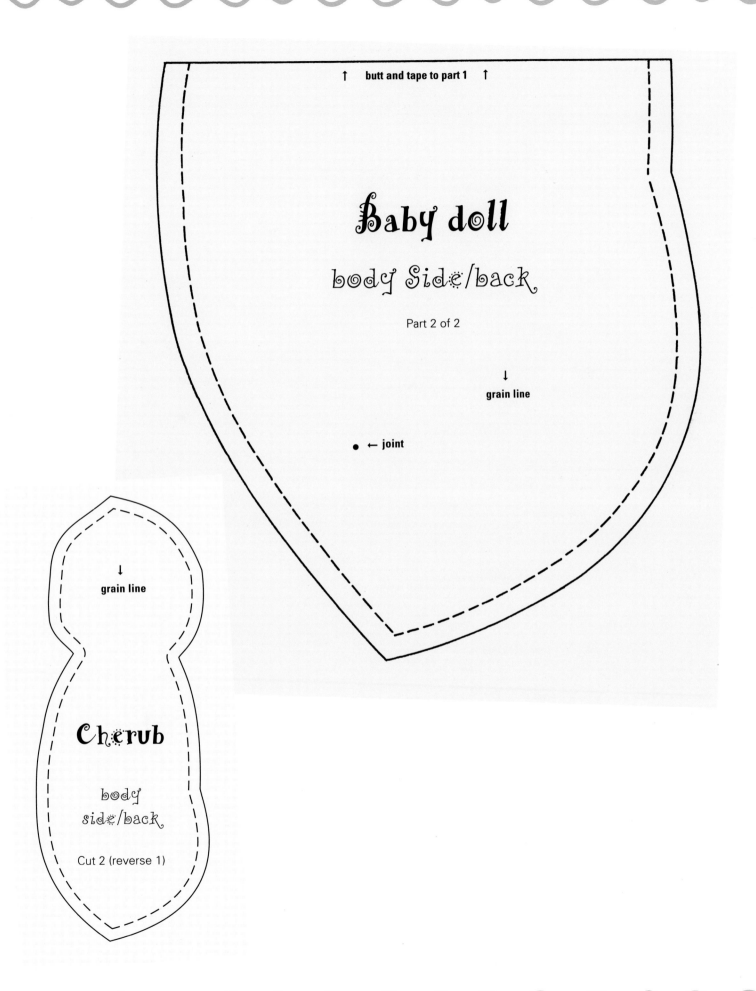

↑   butt and tape to part 1   ↑

Baby doll

body side/back

Part 2 of 2

↓
grain line

● ← **joint**

↓
grain line

Cherub

body
side/back

Cut 2 (reverse 1)

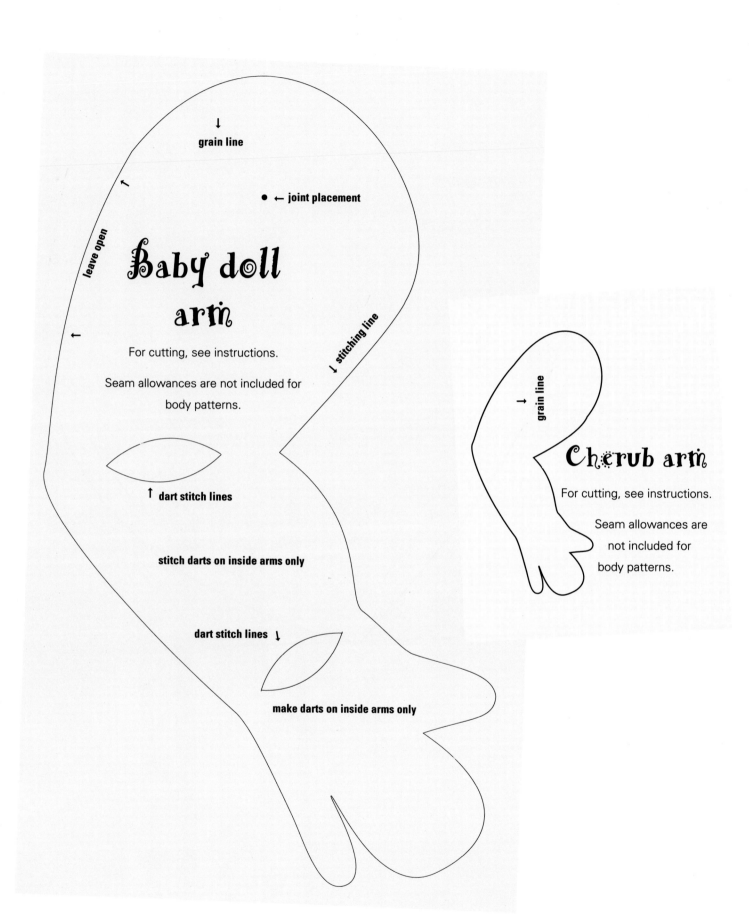

grain line

← joint placement

leave open

Baby doll arm

For cutting, see instructions.

Seam allowances are not included for body patterns.

stitching line

↑ dart stitch lines

stitch darts on inside arms only

dart stitch lines ↓

make darts on inside arms only

grain line

Cherub arm

For cutting, see instructions.

Seam allowances are not included for body patterns.

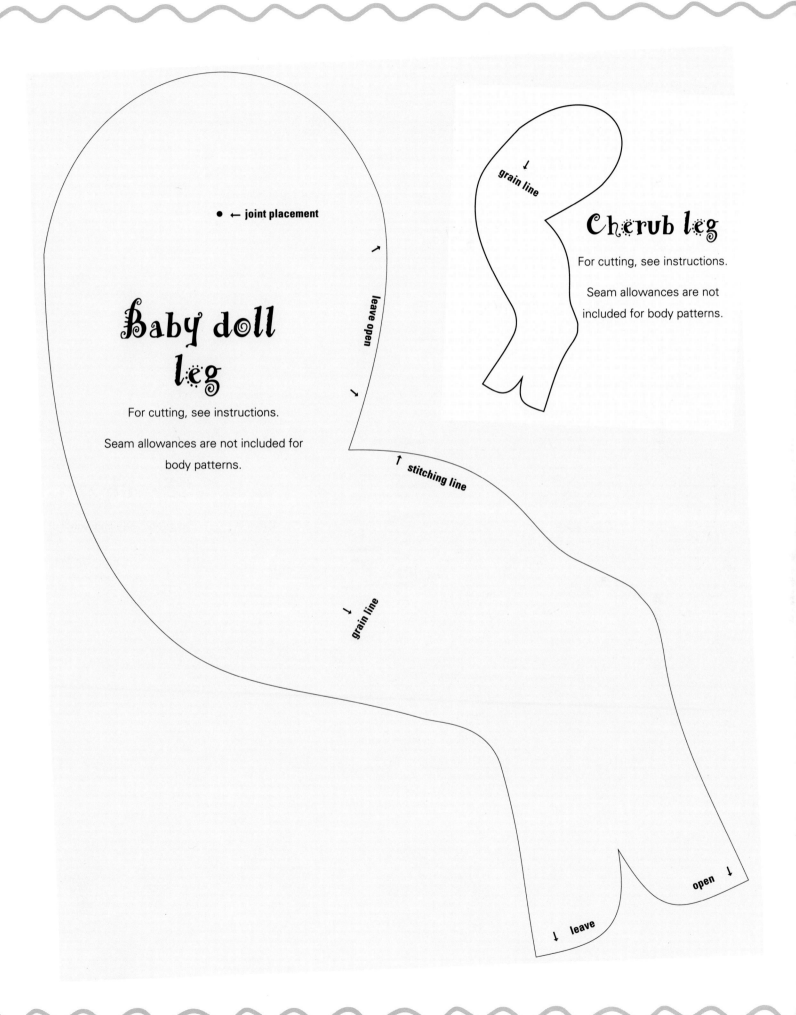

● ← joint placement

Baby doll leg

For cutting, see instructions.

Seam allowances are not included for body patterns.

↑
leave open

↑ stitching line

↓ grain line

↓ leave

open ↓

Cherub leg

For cutting, see instructions.

Seam allowances are not included for body patterns.

↓ grain line

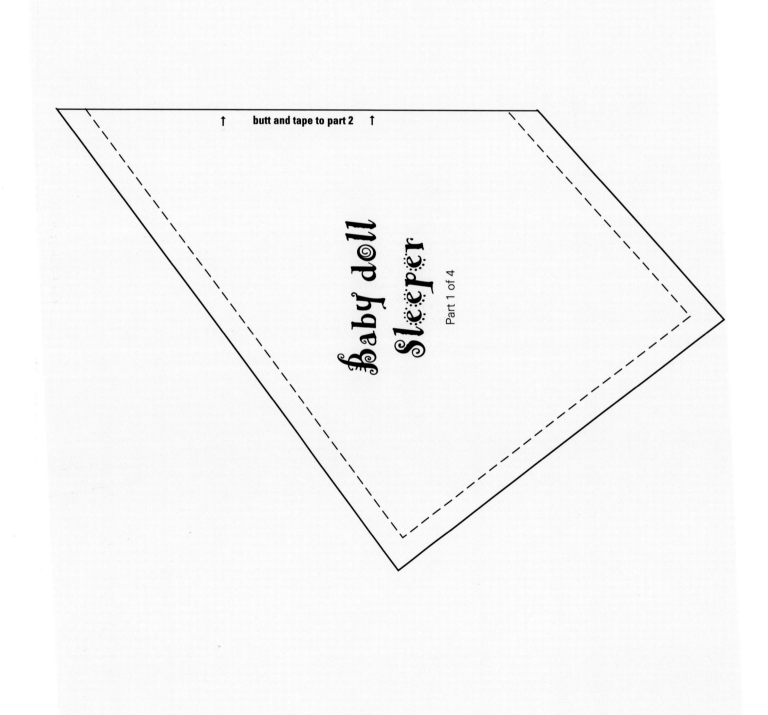

↑   butt and tape to part 2   ↑

Baby doll
Sleeper

Part 1 of 4

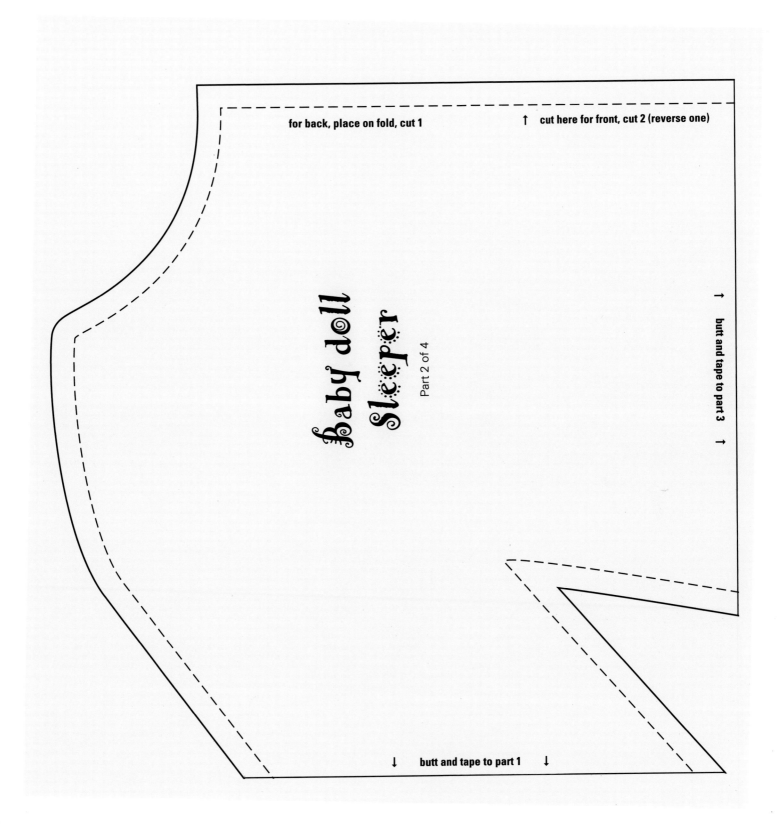

for back, place on fold, cut 1   ↑   cut here for front, cut 2 (reverse one)

Baby doll Sleeper

Part 2 of 4

↑
butt and tape to part 3
↑

↓   butt and tape to part 1   ↓

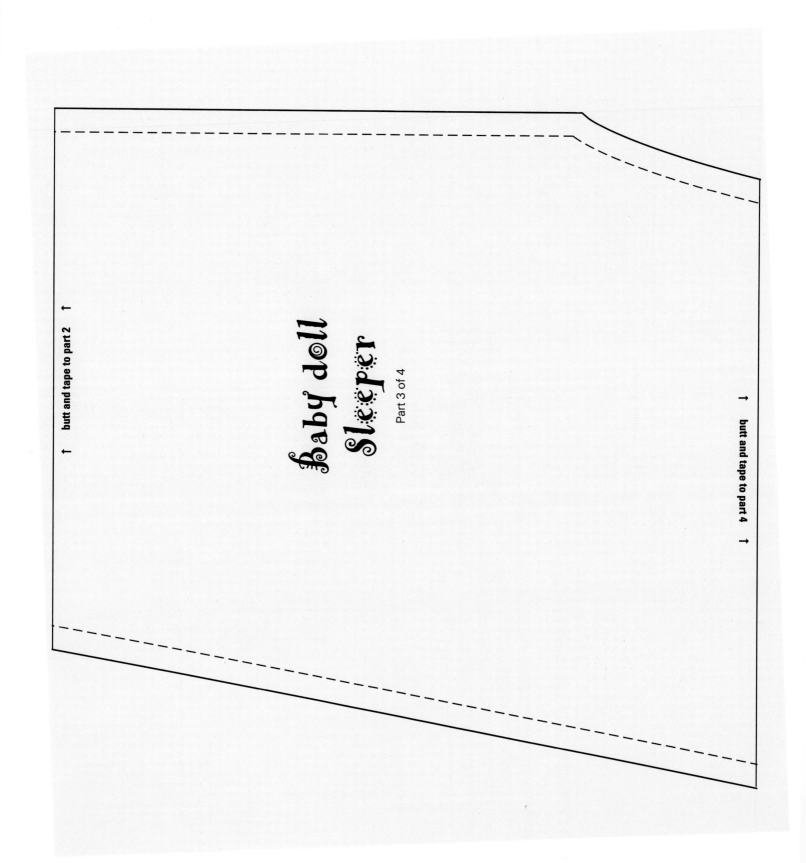

butt and tape to part 2 ↑

↑

Baby doll
Sleeper

Part 3 of 4

↑
butt and tape to part 4
↑

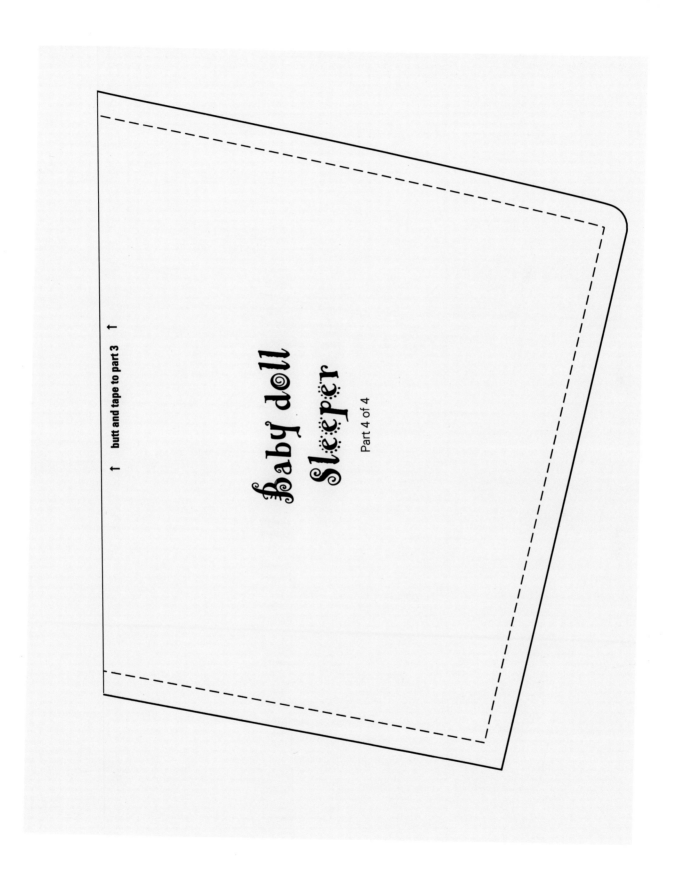

butt and tape to part 3

baby doll
Sleeper

Part 4 of 4

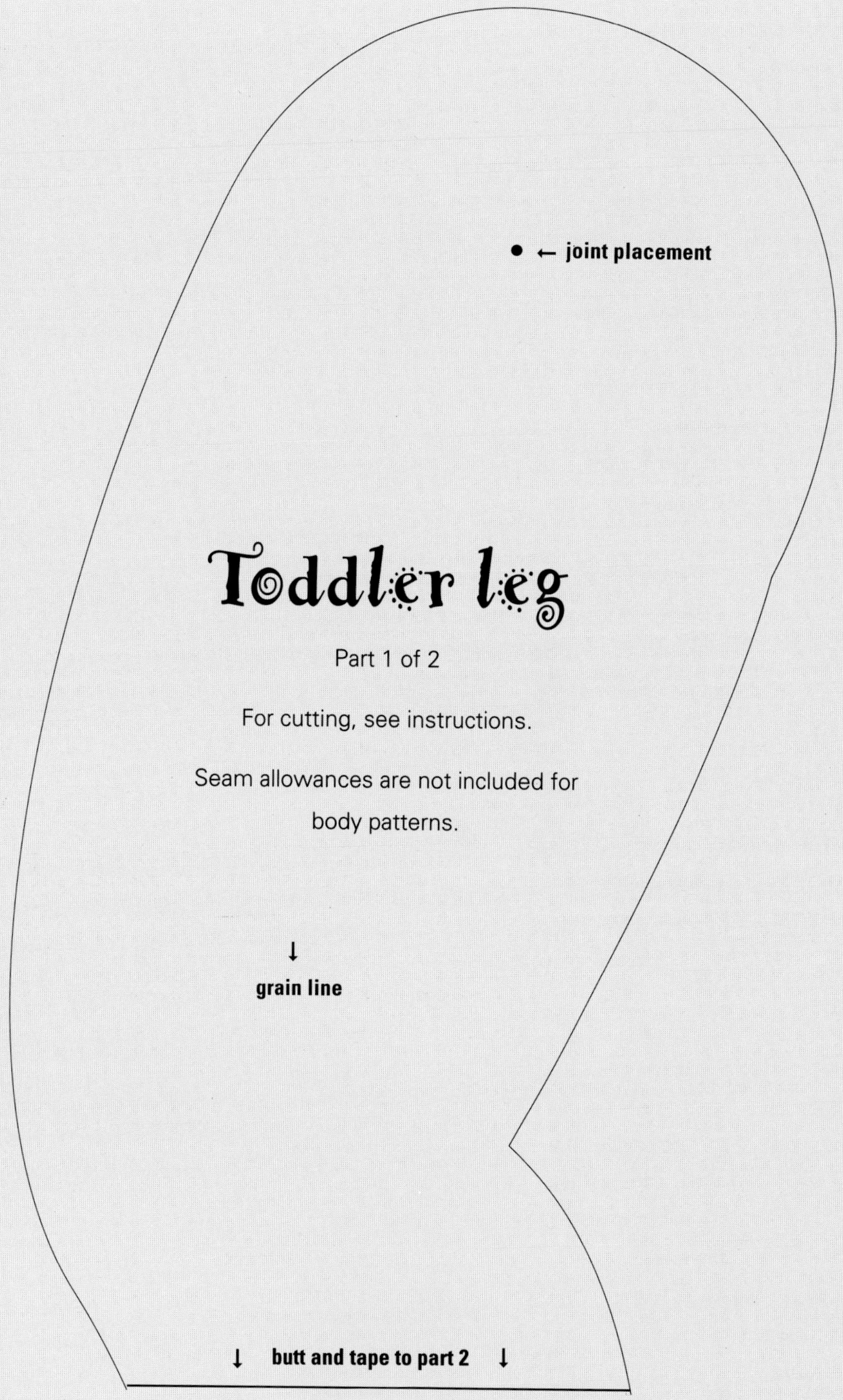

● ← **joint placement**

Toddler leg

Part 1 of 2

For cutting, see instructions.

Seam allowances are not included for
body patterns.

↓

grain line

↓   **butt and tape to part 2**   ↓

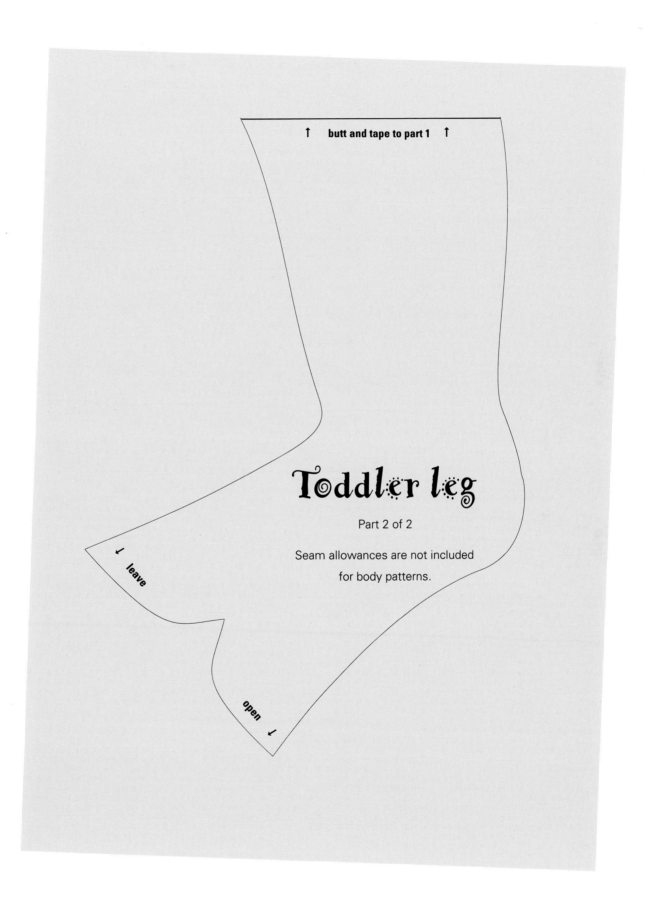

↑ **butt and tape to part 1** ↑

Toddler leg

Part 2 of 2

Seam allowances are not included
for body patterns.

↙ **leave**

open ↙

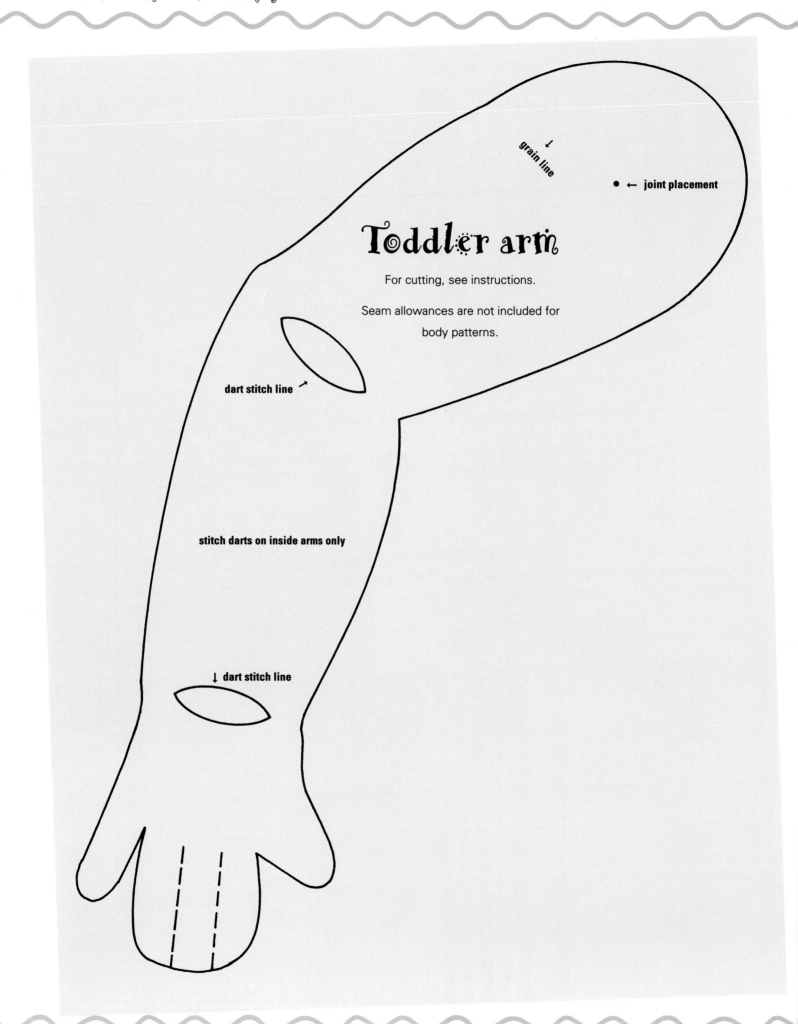

grain line

● ← joint placement

Toddler arm

For cutting, see instructions.

Seam allowances are not included for body patterns.

dart stitch line ↗

stitch darts on inside arms only

↓ dart stitch line

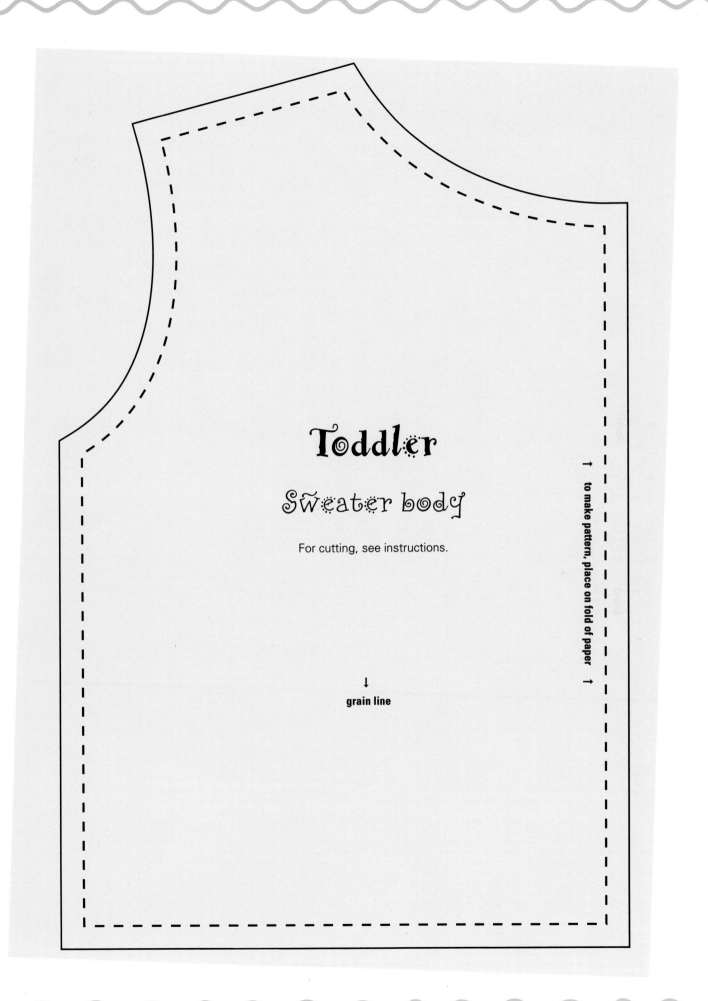

Toddler

Sweater body

For cutting, see instructions.

↓

grain line

→ to make pattern, place on fold of paper →

Baby doll

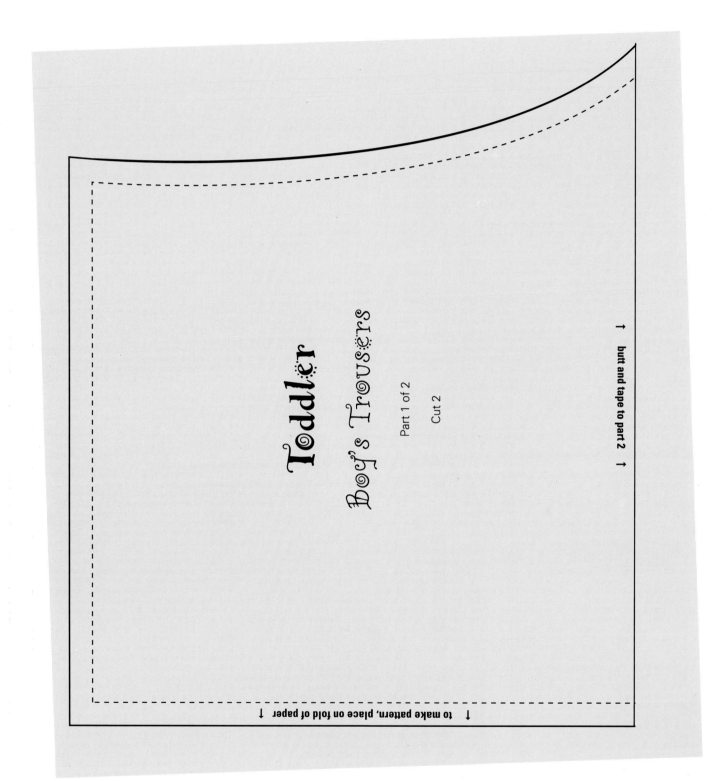

Toddler

Boy's Trousers

Part 1 of 2

Cut 2

butt and tape to part 2

to make pattern, place on fold of paper

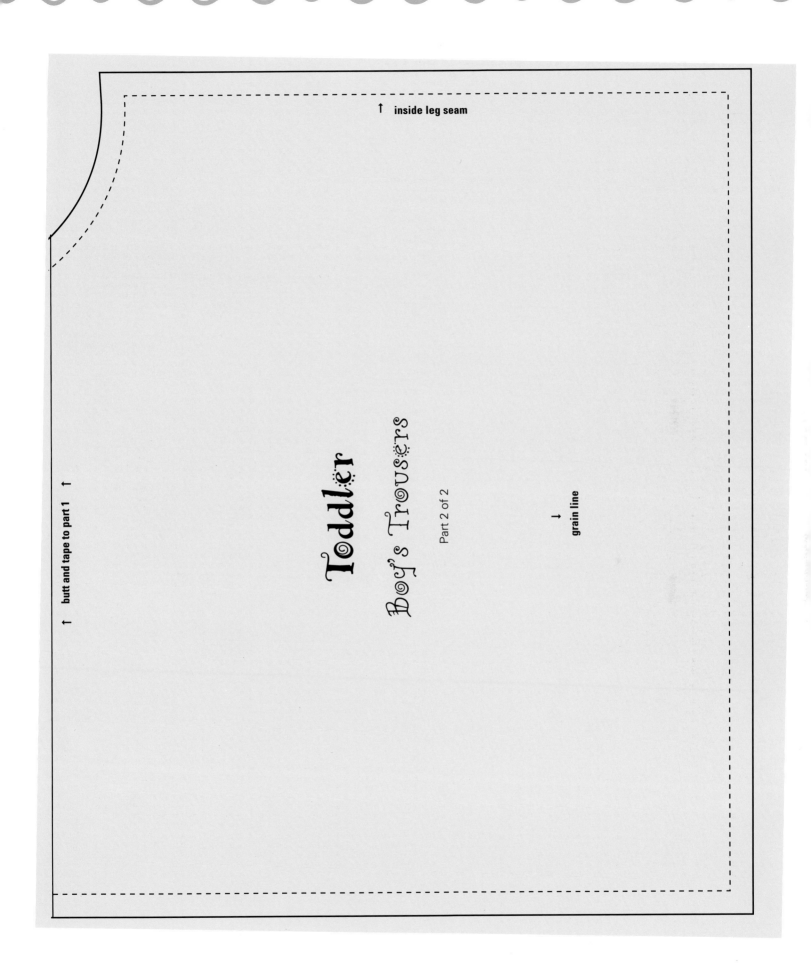

inside leg seam

butt and tape to part 1

Toddler

Boy's Trousers

Part 2 of 2

grain line

Baby doll

Toddler Hat

Cut 2 (1 is lining)

to make pattern,

place on fold of paper

Toddler Hat

Top

Cut 2 (1 is lining)

↑ to make pattern, place on fold of paper ↑

chapter 6

Fashion doll

Our final project builds on the skills attained in creating the four preceding dolls. As a final challenge, making this elegant doll calls for a few more advanced techniques. The reward: a sophisticated fashion doll, ready to don a splendid costume.

The doll's head is sewn separately from the body and attached after stuffing. Thanks to a center seam in the head, this doll has a nose.

The doll's arms and legs are also sewn onto her body after stuffing. The arms can be sewn into any position. With no awkward joints to disguise, this doll can wear revealing clothes: a little evening dress or a bikini. I have included patterns for both a bridal gown and a chic chemise-type dress.

This doll is made with an armature that is attached to a stand. If you prefer to make the doll without a stand, turn to chapter 3, page 32, for instructions on how to insert the armature and stuff the doll.

Finished size: 23 inches (57.5cm) tall

Materials

Body

¹/₂ yard (45cm) of muslin

Matching thread

Polyester fiberfill stuffing

One skein Ironstone English Mohair yarn (I used color #832; see Sources, page 124)

Paints, pencils, pens, or embroidery floss for face

armature

4¹/₂-inch (11.5cm) piece of ³/₈- or ¹/₂-inch (9 or 12mm) plastic tubing

8 feet (2.4m) of aluminum or copper wire (this should be stiff, but bendable)

Tape

White chenille stems

Wooden base

Wedding dress

³/₄ yard (68cm) of bridal satin

Matching thread

¹/₂ yard (45cm) of lace trim for neck edge

1¹/₂ yards (1.3m) of ⁷/₈-inch (2cm) -wide ribbon for sleeve edges

1 yard (90cm) of 2-inch (5cm) -wide ribbon for veil bow

⁵/₈ yard (57cm) of 45- or 60-inch (1.1 or 1.5m) -wide lace fabric for veil

Dried or silk flowers for bouquet

4-inch (10cm) -wide doily for bouquet

Chemise dress

¹/₂ yard (45cm) of dress fabric

Matching thread

Bias binding

Hook and eye

instructions for Fashion doll

1 Prepare the patterns as instructed on pages 12 and 13. Cut the body pieces.

2 Stitch the darts in the body backs. Trim the seam allowances to ¹/₈ inch (3mm).

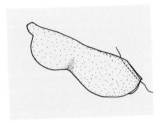

3 Stitch the back seam from neck edge to bottom, leaving an opening between the dots as indicated on the pattern. Trim the seam allowances to ¹/₈ inch (3mm).

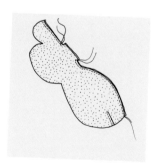

4 Matching the notches, pin and stitch the top fronts to the bottom fronts. Trim the seam allowances to ¹/₈ inch (3mm).

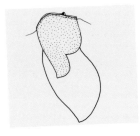

5 Match and pin the two body fronts together along the center front seam. Stitch. Trim the seam allowances to ⅛ inch (3mm).

6 Match and pin the body front to the body back. Stitch all the way around. Trim seam allowances to ⅛ inch (3mm).

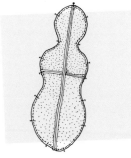

7 As a guide to the ladderstitching you'll do later, mark the stitching lines on the right side of the fabric along the seam lines at the opening at the body back. Apply Fray Check to the raw

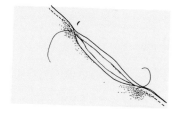

edges at the back opening. Allow to dry. Turn the body right side out.

8 Stitch the front and then the back of the leg, from top to bottom. Trim the seam allowances to ⅛ inch (3mm). Repeat for the second leg.

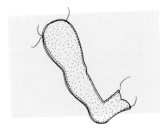

9 Fold the leg so the front and back seams match at the toe. Stitch across the toes. Trim the seam allowances to

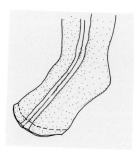

⅛ inch (3mm). Turn right side out. Repeat for the remaining leg.

10 To make the left leg, lay the leg down so that the toes point to the left. Position the leg pattern on top of the leg, matching the top and side edges. Trace the bottom curved line at the top of the leg to the muslin.

Repeat for the right leg, making sure that the toes point to the right.

Cut along the traced lines. These are the insides of the leg. Repeat for the other leg. Turn the legs right side out.

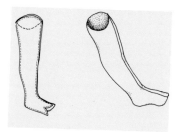

11 **Note:** The arm pattern does not include a seam allowance.

Lay the arm pattern on the muslin and trace around it. Stitch just inside the traced line, all the way around the arm. Trim the extra fabric outside of the stitching to a ⅛-inch (3mm) seam allowance. Cut to the stitching between the fingers. Repeat for the second arm.

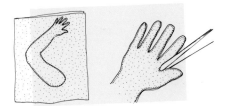

12 Hold the arms together. Make 1-inch (2.5cm) -long slashes on the sides of the arms that face one another. Slashes will be at the inside of the arms, hidden against the shoulders of

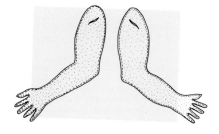

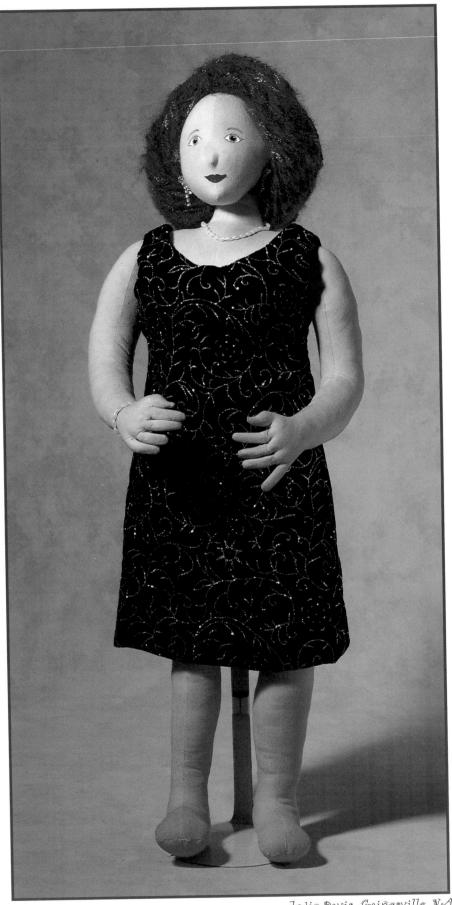

Jodie Davis, Gainesville, VA

the doll. Apply Fray Check to the raw edges of the slashes. Allow to dry.

13 Apply Fray Check to the seam allowances between the fingers. Turn them while the Fray Check is still wet. Insert opened hemostats into the arm. Push the slightly opened tip of the jaws against the end of one finger. Push the fabric at the tip of the finger into the jaws. Close the jaws.

Pull the finger gently into the palm (see page 50). Repeat for the other fingers. Grab several fingers with the hemostats and pull the arm right side out. Push the fingers and seams out smoothly with the Stuff-It™ tool.

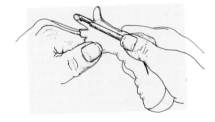

14 Match the two head fronts along the center front edges. Stitch the center front of the face. Trim the seam allowances to ⅛ inch (3mm).

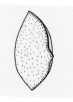

15 Pin the head front to the head back, right sides together. Match the seams to the dots on the head back. Stitch all the way around. Trim the seam allowances to ⅛ inch (3mm).

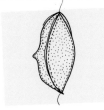

16 Transfer the slash mark at the head back to the fabric. Slash the head back. Apply Fray Check. Allow to dry. Turn right side out.

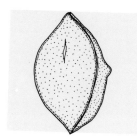

17 If not making an armature, proceed to step 18.

To make an armature, cut a piece of wire 6 feet (1.8m) long. Bend in half. Twist the wire about 2 inches (5cm) below the bend. Insert the plastic tubing into the twist 1½ inches (4cm) below the top bend of the wire. Twist the wire about 6 more inches (15cm) below the plastic tubing. Bend each

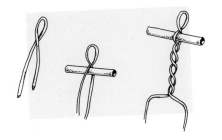

end of the wire approximately 2 inches out to the side and down again. Leave the remaining wire free. Make holes for the armature in the body at the markings. Apply Fray Check.

Insert the leg ends of the armature into the opening at the back of the body and out through the holes in the bottom of the body. Work the top of the armature into place.

Stuff the top ½ inch (12mm) of the neck and the bottom 1½ inches (4cm) of the body. Adjust the armature so that the bend at the top butts up to the stuffing in the neck. Continue stuffing the bottom of the body, adding pieces around the leg wires and encasing the hip in the center of the stuffing. Keep checking to be sure the armature has not slipped out of the neck. Stuff the neck and the shoulders, encasing the plastic shoulder tubing in the center of the body. Finish stuffing the body.

18 For a doll without an armature, stuff the body (see pages 20 and 67 for more information on stuffing).

19 For the armature, make holes at the markings at the bottoms of the feet. Apply Fray Check. Allow to dry.

20 Stuff the toes of either doll.

21 For the armature, slide one leg onto the appropriate leg wire. Pull the leg up almost to the finished position. Bend the wire below the bottom of the foot. This will keep the leg from sliding off the wire as you stuff it.

22 Stuff the foot, then the ankle. If using an armature, place pieces of stuffing one at a time around the wire, encasing the wire in the center of the leg. Stuff the leg to about 3 inches (7cm) below the top. Don't worry if the leg faces the wrong direction. You can right it before you stitch it to the body.

23 Fold the raw edge at the top of the leg about ¼ inch (6mm) to the wrong side. Match the back seam of the leg to the dart at the back of the body. Pin. Pin the outside half of the

top of the leg to the doll. Hand stitch using a small backstitch.

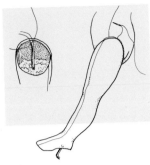

24 Stuff the top of the leg through the opening at the inside of the leg. Turn under ¼ inch (6mm) at the top of the remaining raw edge of the top of the leg and pin to the body. The top of the leg at the inside will be about ½ inch (12mm) from the center body seam at the crotch. Finish hand stitching the leg to the body. If necessary, insert a little more stuffing before you make the last stitches.

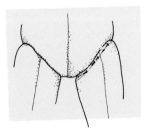

25 For a doll with no armature, proceed to step 26.

For armatured hands and arms: cut five chenille stems in half. Match two pieces. Fold them in half. Insert them, folded end first, into a finger. Repeat for all five fingers. You may find it easier to insert the chenille stems with the hemostats.

Fold back the arm so it is wrong side out, exposing the ends of the chenille stems. Cut a piece of armature wire about 1 foot (30cm) long. Gather together the ends of the chenille stems. Insert the armature wire into the center of them. Wrap tape around the stems and the wire.

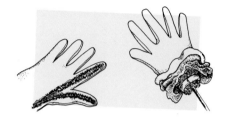

Work the arm fabric up the armature wire to turn it right side out again. About ½ inch (12mm) from the top of the arm, bend the wire out perpendicular from the arm so you can insert it into the shoulder and the plastic shoulder tube. Cut the protruding wire to 3 inches (7cm) in length.

26 For a doll with an armature: Put a bit of stuffing in the jaws of the hemostats. Insert into the thumb. Push it into the bend of the thumb with the closed tips of the hemostat or a stuffing tool. Add another piece of stuffing

to fill the thumb. Insert bits of stuffing into the base of each finger, top and bottom, to fill them out and smooth the fabric, which will want to fold and bunch there.

For arms without the armature: Use the hemostats to insert small bits of stuffing into each finger. You may find it easier to twist the stuffing into a tiny tube first. After the fingers are stuffed, stuff the palm. Make sure the transition from finger to palm is smooth. Otherwise unstuff the palm and insert more stuffing into the bases of the fingers.

For arms with or without an armature, continue stuffing the arm up to the top. Leave the top of the arm lightly stuffed.

For the armature, push the wire through the hole in the shoulder of the body. Put the fingers of your free hand inside the doll to feel through the stuffing for the end of the plastic tube. Push the wire into the plastic tube.

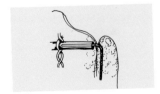

For arms with or without an armature, place the arm in the desired position. Stuff the arm so it is smooth from body to shoulder. Pin and stitch the top half of the arm to the doll's body along the seam.

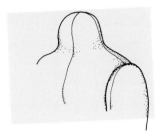

27 If you haven't embroidered the face already, this is a good time to do so, before the head is attached to the doll.

28 Stuff the top of the head almost down to the nose. To keep the stuffing from migrating out of the nose, push the seam allowances of the nose out through the back opening of the head. Apply a small amount of glue to the seam allowances from the bottom to the top of the nose. Push the nose back in place. Stuff a kidney bean–size piece of stuffing into the nose. Push in firmly with the closed end of the hemostats or your stuffing tool. Do the same for the chin. Finish stuffing the

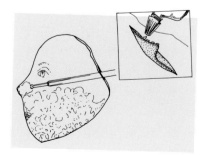

head. Whipstitch (see page 21) the slash at the back of the head closed.

29 Cut a 3-inch (7cm) -square piece of body fabric. Right sides together, fold in half. Stitch along the raw edges. Make a slash at one end. Turn right side out. This will be the back head tab, which will secure the back of the head to the neck.

30 With the slashed side of the tab facing the back of the neck, stitch the bottom ½ inch (12mm) of the tab to the neck.

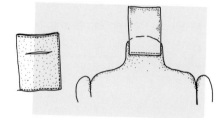

31 Pin the bottom of the head to the front of the neck. Pin the remainder of the neck tab to the back of the head. Stitch. Remove the pins. Stitch the back of the doll's head, behind the chin, to the neck.

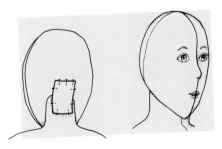

32 Hand stitch the chin to the neck.

hair

1 Place the unopened hank of yarn against the back of the doll's head to see how you need to manipulate it to cover the head. Remove. Holding the yarn with your thumbs on top and remaining fingers underneath, work the yarn underneath so that the hank becomes more like an upside-down bowl, making it a bit larger to cover the head. Put the wig on the doll's head. Keep working the wig until it fits the head.

2 While holding the wig in place, lift sections in turn and apply hot or tacky glue to the doll's head. Press the wig to the head.

Wedding dress

1 Stitch the darts in the bodice front and bodice front lining pieces. Press the darts away from the center.

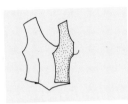

2 Stitch the bodice front to the bodice backs at the shoulder and side seams. Press the seams open. Repeat for the lining.

3 With right sides together, stitch the lining to the bodice at back and neck edges. Turn right side out. Press.

4 Stitch sleeve seams. Press open.

5 At the lower edge of each sleeve, press ¼ inch (6mm) to the wrong side. Repeat.

6 Gather the top edge of the sleeves between the dots.

7 Match the dots on the sleeves to those on the bodice armhole edges. Treating the two layers of the bodice as one, pin the sleeves to the armholes, pulling up the gathering to fit. Stitch.

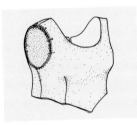

8 Cut a 15- by 44-inch (37.5 by 112cm) (or the width of the fabric) rectangle from the bridal satin for the skirt. Fold the rectangle in half and finger-press to mark the center. Unfold.

9 Lay the front triangle cut-out template on top of this line, with the fabric fold matching the line on the pattern.

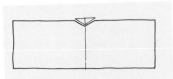

Trace the angled line onto the fabric. Remove the pattern and cut the triangle out of the fabric. This is the top edge of the skirt.

10 Fold the skirt in half, right sides together, matching the short side edges. Beginning at the top edge and using a ½-inch (12mm) seam allowance, start with a basting stitch from the top edge. Halfway down the seam, switch to a normal stitch length. Backstitch. Continue stitching to the bottom edge. Press the seam open.

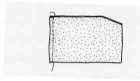

11 Turn both seam allowances ¼ inch (6mm) to the wrong side. From the right side, topstitch a scant ¼ inch from the center seam along both sides. Remove the basting stitches.

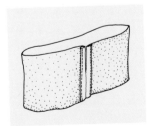

Jodie Davis, Gainesville, VA

12 Beginning and ending 2 inches (5cm) from the center back, gather the top edge of the skirt.

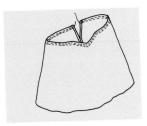

13 Matching the back edges and treating the bodice and bodice lining as one, pin the skirt to the bodice. Match the point at the bodice front to the point of the triangle on the skirt. Pull up on the gathering stitches to fit. Pin. Stitch.

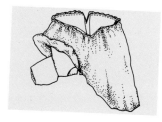

14 Press ¼ inch (6mm) to the wrong side along the lower edge of the skirt for the hem. Repeat. Topstitch the hem.

15 Put the dress on the doll. If the clothing will be removed frequently, sew snaps to fasten the dress back. Otherwise, slipstitch the back closed. If desired, sew tiny decorative buttons down the back.

16 Gather the lower edge of the sleeves. Pull up gathers to fit and knot

thread. Cut the ⅞-inch (2cm) -wide ribbon into four pieces. Tie into bows. Trim the ends. Hand stitch the bows to the lower edge of the sleeves.

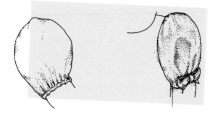

Veil

~~~~~~~~~~~~~~~

1 Fold the long, cut edges of the veil fabric to the front about 2 inches (5cm).

2 Fold the top 18 inches (45cm) to the front, toward you.

3 Gather the lace fabric 2 inches (5cm) below the fold. Pull up on the gathering to make this section 3½ inches (9cm) wide. Tie the ends of the thread to secure. If desired, use a regular machine stitch over the basting to secure.

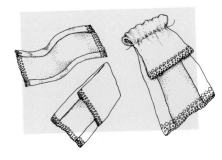

4 Make a bow with the 2-inch (5cm) -wide ribbon. Stitch to the center of the gathered section. Trim the ribbon ends at an angle.

5 Stitch the veil to the doll's head through the wig.

Bouquet

~~~~~~~~~~~~~~~

1 Gather the flowers into a bunch. Wrap a doily around them. Stitch to secure.

2 Bend the doll's arms to hold the bouquet. Tack the bouquet to the doll's hands.

Chemise dress

1 **Optional:** Stitch the darts in the dress fronts.

2 Using a ½-inch (6mm) seam allowance, baste the center back of the dress from the neck to 5 inches (12.5cm) below the neck. Switch to a regular stitch. Backstitch. Continue stitching to the bottom of the dress.

3 Press the seam open. Press the seam allowance ¼ inch (6mm) to the wrong side. Topstitch.

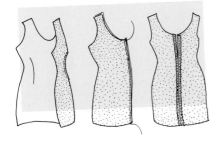

4 With right sides together, stitch the dress front to the dress backs at the shoulders and sides.

5 Stitch the bias binding to the neck and armhole edges, right sides together. Fold the binding to the wrong side. Topstitch by machine or slipstitch by hand in place.

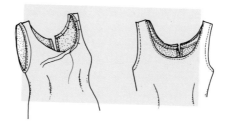

6 Hem the dress to the desired length. Sew a hook and eye to the top at back neck.

making Faces

More than any other detail, the face is what makes a doll. No matter how beautifully clothed, how carefully stitched and stuffed, or how artistically posed, a poorly made face will ruin a doll. No wonder face making is seen as the most challenging aspect of doll-making. You can choose from a variety of mediums: paint, embroidery, crayon, or colored pencil. Use the technique with which you feel most comfortable.

If you are uncomfortable with all of these, then use appliquéd fabric features (see pages 33–34). Easier still, use buttons, sequins, or beads. Please remember, however, that if you are using these additions, the doll is not suitable for children under three years of age.

Some dollmakers prefer to make a face before constructing the doll. This way, if you're unhappy with the face you made, you need only discard a piece of fabric, not a completed doll.

Other dollmakers create the faces after stitching and stuffing the doll. This is the preferred method for a freehand face because it is difficult to judge where to place the face on the flat fabric.

Either way, making doll faces requires practice. You will find the time you spend making several sample

Linda Hargan, Elk Grove, CA

faces worthwhile. If you leave enough fabric around each, you can make dolls from the successful faces. No one will know how many tries it took to get just the right expression.

"Before adding features to the face I go over the lines with a fine tip permanent marker. This way I can better see what I'm doing."

Jodie Davis
Gainesville, VA

Colorwash

Applied before painting the features, a colorwash can color the entire face and even the body or can be as simple as soft shading. These highlights—a soft tinting above the eyes, a hint of color for the cheeks, or a light shading along the nose—add depth and realism to the face.

To apply a colorwash, mix textile medium with acrylic paint or dye. Test the mixture on a scrap of the doll body fabric. Add more textile medium until

you reach the desired tint. The textile medium, available at craft stores, extends the color without running.

The colorwash can be applied just around the eyes, nose, cheeks, and mouth, or over the entire face. In the latter case I also colorwash the body parts which may be exposed: the hands, lower arms, feet, and lower legs.

For a soft effect, apply plain textile medium to the fabric before using the paint/medium mixture. Don't worry if the fabric seems quite wet.

Jodie Davis, Gainesville, VA

Jodie Davis, Gainesville, VA

As when applying makeup, successful colorwashing involves blending. If I'm using a light brown on the face I increase the darkness a bit around the nose and eyes. After I apply the pink cheek color I dip my brush in plain medium, or a light brown tinted medium, and gently scrub the edges of the cheeks to blend them into the skin color. If I find I've applied too much color I blend it out with pure medium. If you need to remove some color, just dab or scrub softly with a paper towel.

Strong coffee or tea gives an antique look. I dunked an entire rag doll, painted face and all, in tea, then left her in a sunny spot on the porch for a few days to dry.

Remember, whatever method you choose, allow the colorwash to dry before painting the face.

Painting

Think of painting as a matter of layering, beginning at the bottom and working up.

I use a small brush (#0) for face painting. Toothpicks are useful for making dots and drawing tiny lines. I usually apply two coats of paint to the face, beginning with the whites of the eyes. When the first coat is nearly dry I add a second. Next I apply the eye color. I almost always have to mix paint to get just the right shade. Paint taken out of the tube or jar is too flat for a natural look. Too bright a blue might require a drop of brown, for instance, or you may have to add a dash of yellow to cheer up a dark brown.

For the second coat I like to add a little variety. For blue eyes I add tiny

Barbara Stansbury, Washington, DC

radiating stripes of a darker and a lighter blue. Brown eyes get darker brown and gold highlight stripes.

When the iris is nearly dry I paint black pupils. Start with a dot in the center and work out, enlarging it into a circle. The semimoist eye color will mix with the black pupil color around the edges for a realistic look.

While the eyes dry I paint the mouth. I've found it easier to paint from the inside out. Otherwise everything ends up too big. Again, paint one coat, let it dry, and add another. I use a lighter shade along the top of the bottom lip and at the center third of the top lip. I either paint the line between the lips or draw it in with permanent marker after the mouth has dried.

By now the pupil should be dry. Using a toothpick or tiny brush, add two white highlights to each pupil.

Go over the eyelashes, eyebrows, and drawn lines for the eyes and nose with paint or a fine-tip permanent marker.

To make freckles, dot the upper cheeks with reddish brown paint using a toothpick or a fine-tip marker.

For a fun effect, apply glitter paint to the doll's face. This paint looks like white paste in the jar. Once dry it

becomes totally clear and the sparkles appear. I add some to eyelids, brows, and cheeks.

Makeup

We use makeup for our faces, so why not for our doll's faces?

Denise Roominger, Cranbury, NJ

I use makeup on my dolls the same way I do on my face. Apply eye shadow above the eyes at the outer edges in a V, and a hint of a line below the eyes. Line the eyes with eye pencil.

Blush gives just the right healthy

glow to my doll's cheeks. A piece of tissue is the best applicator. Wrap it around your finger and dab it in the blush. Blot it and test it by gently dabbing it on a scrap of the fabric you used for your doll's face. (The back of the unwigged head is convenient.) Go easy with the blush. Start with much less than you need, then build it up.

Once you have a satisfactory amount of blush on the face, use a fresh piece of tissue to soften the color in the center and blend it into the cheek fabric. In addition to the cheeks, I like to apply a little blush above and between the eyebrows and to the chin.

advanced Painting Skills

My artist friend, the illustrator of this book, Barbara Hennig, gave me a crash course in face painting, which I'm sharing here.

She told me that black doesn't exist in nature. Come to think of it, she's right. Charcoal, blue-black, brown, chestnut, and any flesh tone are fine for drawing doll's faces, but not black.

Likewise, look into a friend's eyes. Do you see a circle? You probably won't, unless he or she is startled.

The top lid covers part of the top of the circular iris.

To give the eyes a lifelike roundness, shade them in three places: the corners of the whites of the eyes, under the top lids, and along the bottom of the iris. For the latter, use a dark shade of the color chosen for the eye color. For the lid and corner shading, use a soft gray art marker, such as the Berol Prismacolor in 10% Warm Gray (see Sources, page 124).

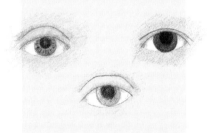

Look again at a real eye, and notice the highlights. No, there isn't a white dot in the center of the pupil. Rather, the highlight is off center, even overlapping onto the iris, and is comprised of two dots.

To help you draw lips, Barbara shares her two-over-one circle trick. She also tells me she draws the lip line before coloring the lips.

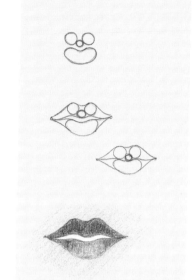

To set the face so it won't smudge, spray it with a fixative, available at an art supply or craft store.

Embroidery

Embroidery is more easily done before stitching the doll together. An embroidery hoop holds the fabric taut, ensuring more even stitches. When I've tried embroidering faces on a finished doll the needle brought fiberfill with it as it emerged from inside the doll.

To transfer the features to the fabric, try a Sulky Iron-On Pen (see Sources, page 124). Available in a range of colors, these pens transfer a clear marking to the fabric. Since you will be embroidering over the marking, it will not show on the finished doll.

Draw the details of the face with a pencil or a dressmaker's marker. Using three or four strands of floss, outline or backstitch the eyebrows.

Satin stitch the eyes and the mouth.

Do not be tempted to carry the thread at the back from one section of the face to another. It will inevitably show through the fabric.

You may wish to use a color-wash before you embroider, or add blush afterwards.

Jodie Davis, Gainesville, VA

Simple embroidery, Buttons, beads

For a no-fail face, search the notions department or the bead aisle of your fabric store for any number of potential doll face materials.

Buttons are a natural for eyes. Try the ideas I have provided or use your own.

A row of small buttons can be stitched into a mouth, or you can use sequins or beads. Using embroidery floss, stitch through a heart-shaped bead for a simple, cute mouth.

Try these goof-proof stitches for an easy embroidered face. Now stitch a sequin or button star on each cheek, or even add a heart-shaped jewel. Please remember that if you are adding buttons or beads to a doll, it cannot be used as a toy for children under three years of age.

appliquéd Face

Turn to chapter 3, pages 33–34, for appliquéd face instructions.

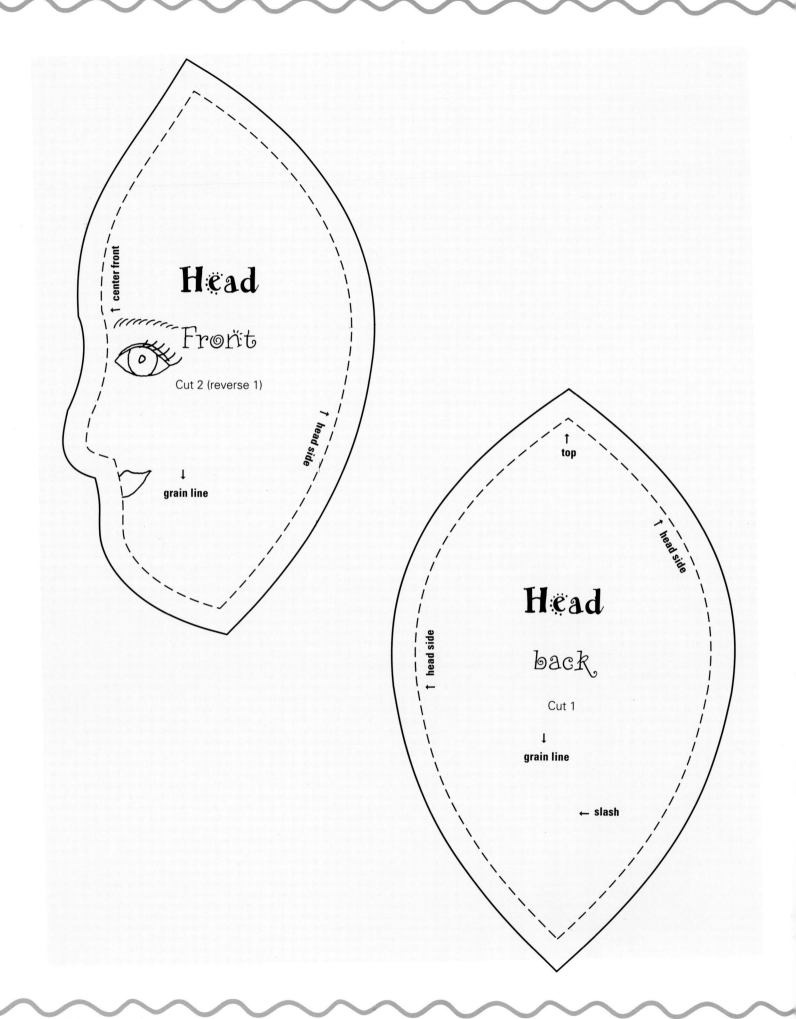

Head

↑ center front

Front

Cut 2 (reverse 1)

↑ head side

↓ grain line

Head

↑ top

↑ head side

↑ head side

back

Cut 1

↓ grain line

← slash

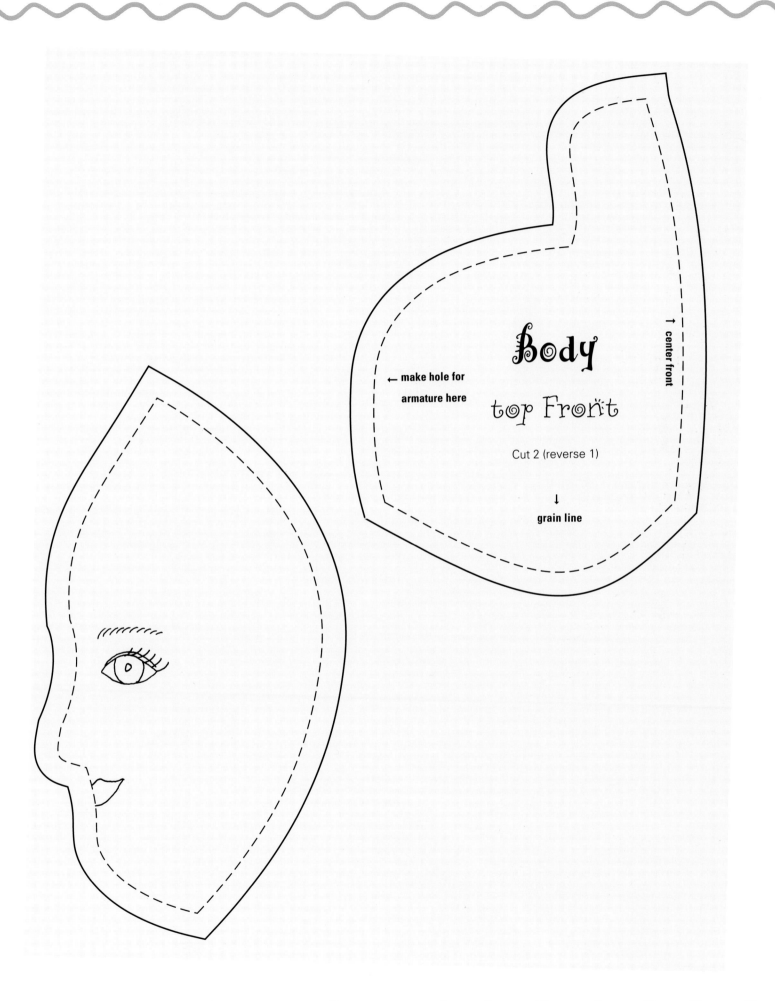

Body

top Front

Cut 2 (reverse 1)

← make hole for armature here

↑ center front

↓

grain line

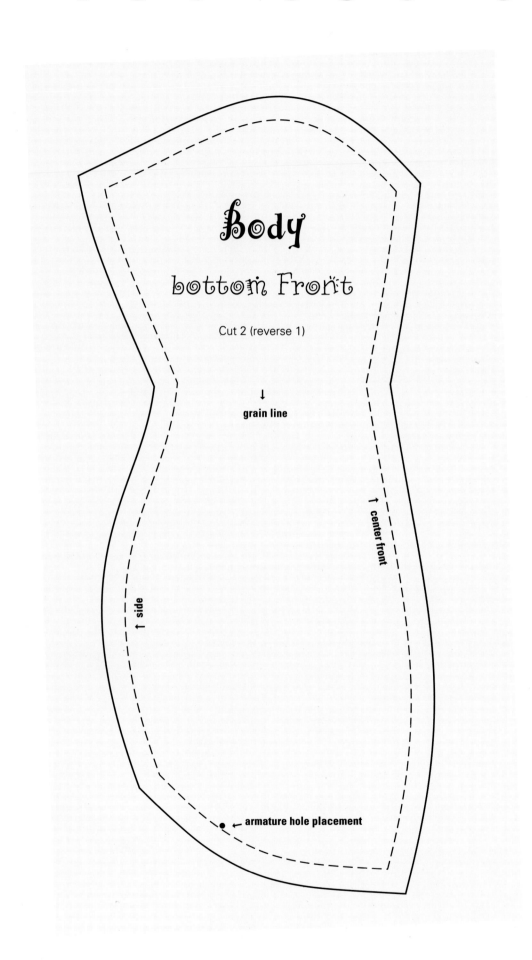

Body

bottom Front

Cut 2 (reverse 1)

↓
grain line

↑ **center front**

↑ **side**

● ← **armature hole placement**

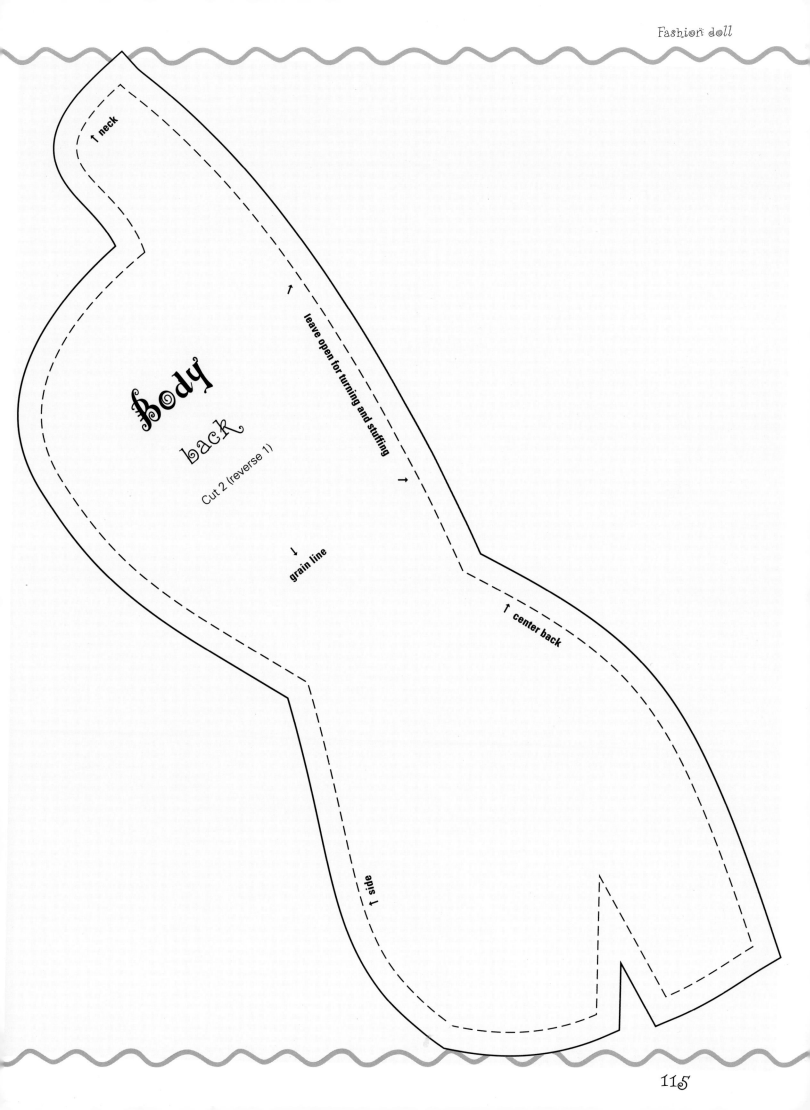

↑ neck

leave open for turning and stuffing

↑

Body

back

Cut 2 (reverse 1)

↑ grain line

↑ center back

↑ side

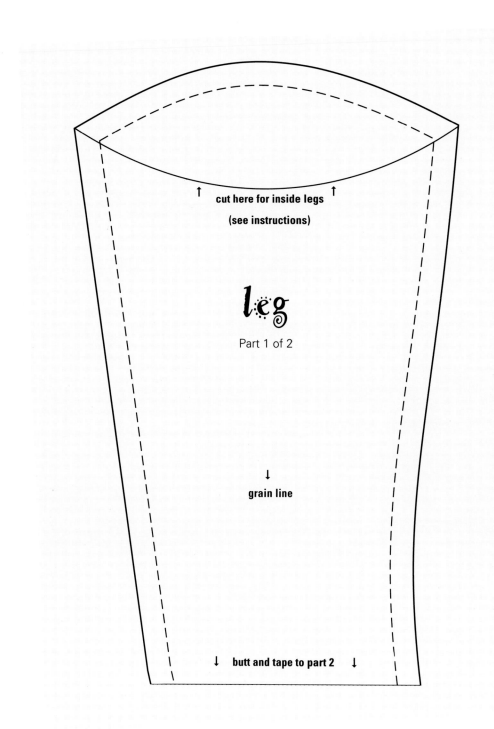

cut here for inside legs

(see instructions)

leg

Part 1 of 2

↓

grain line

↓   butt and tape to part 2   ↓

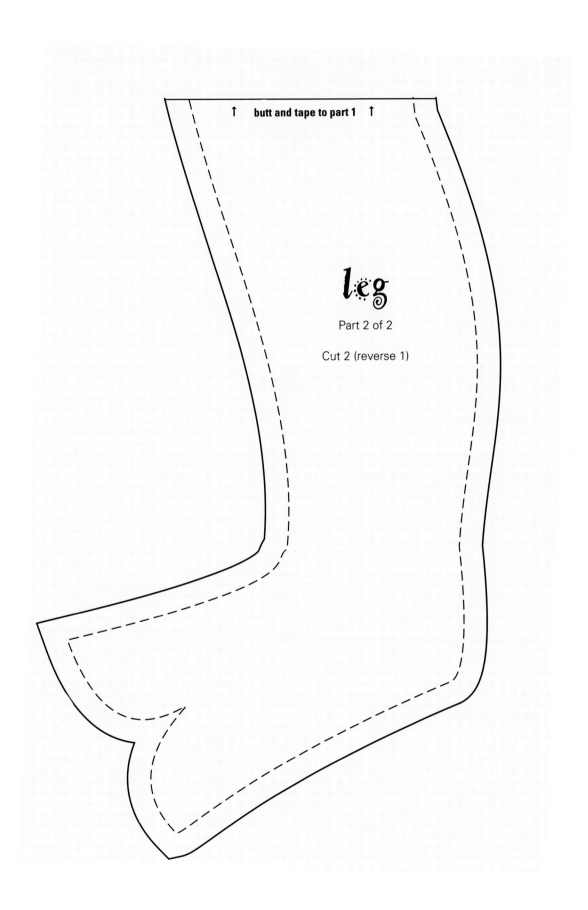

↑ **butt and tape to part 1** ↑

l·e·g

Part 2 of 2

Cut 2 (reverse 1)

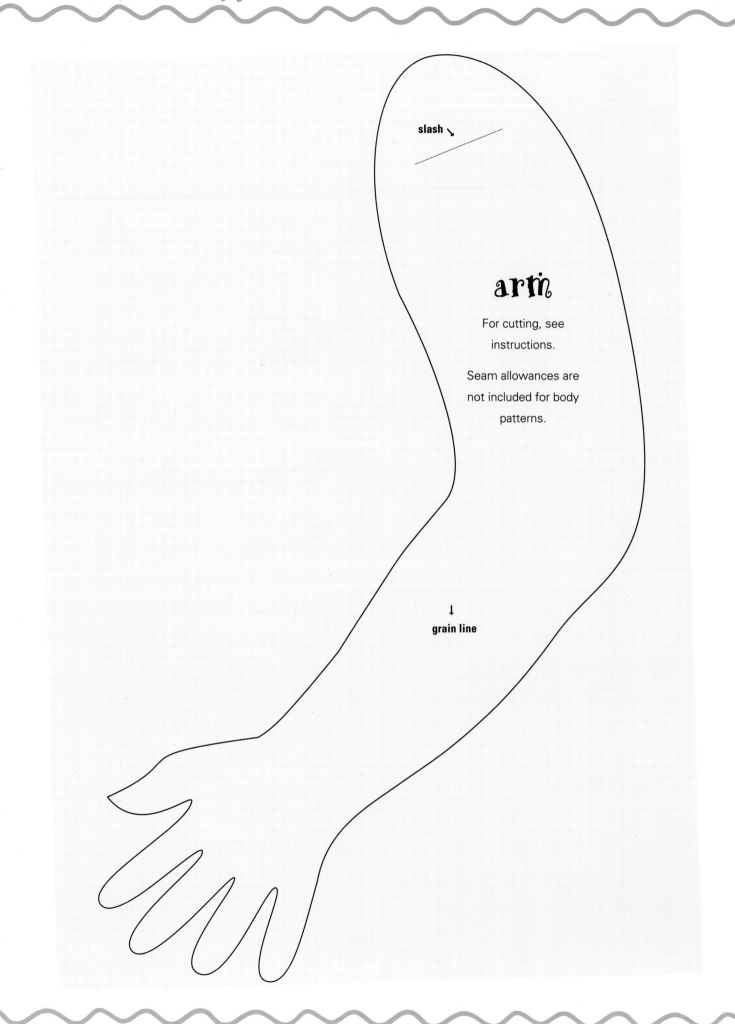

slash ↘

arm

For cutting, see
instructions.

Seam allowances are
not included for body
patterns.

↓
grain line

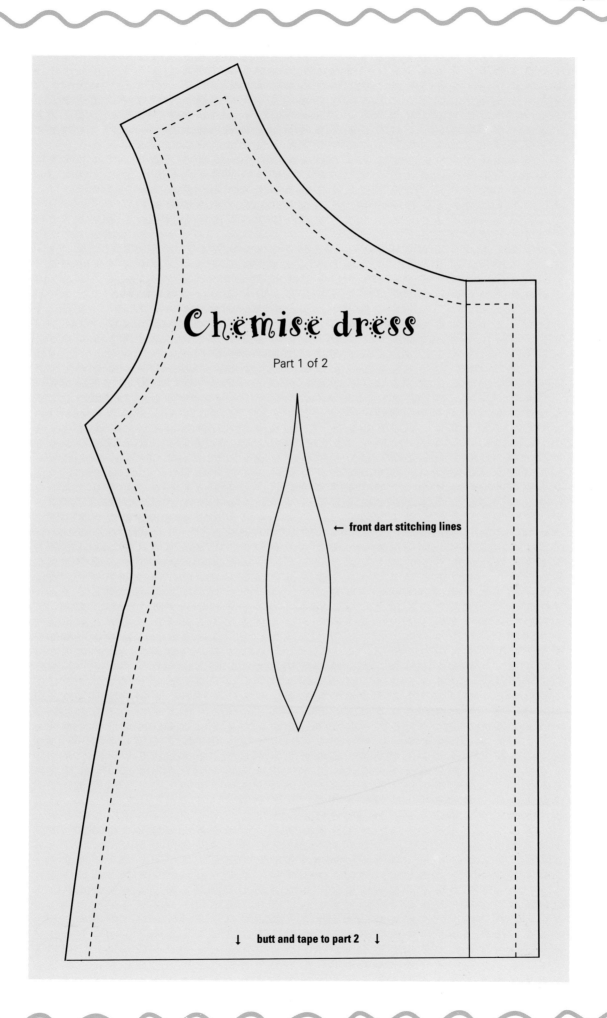

Chemise dress

Part 1 of 2

← **front dart stitching lines**

↓   **butt and tape to part 2**   ↓

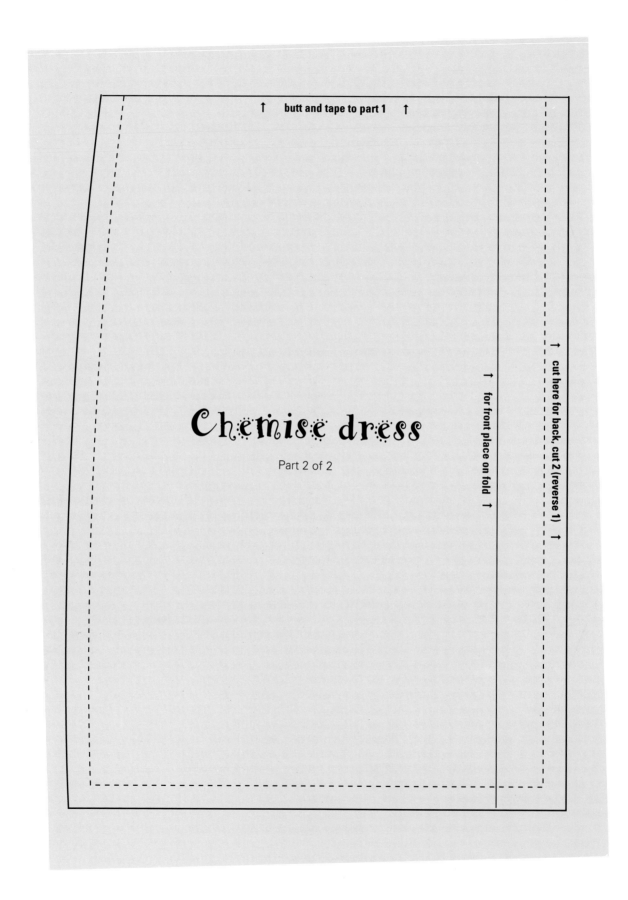

↑   **butt and tape to part 1**   ↑

Chemise dress

Part 2 of 2

↑ for front place on fold ↑

↑ cut here for back, cut 2 (reverse 1) ↑

Bridal Gown

bodice front

Cut 2 (reverse 1)

↓
grain line

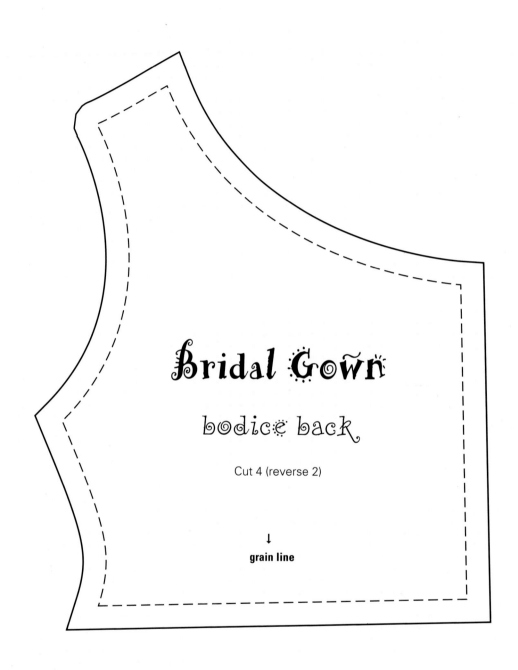

Bridal Gown

bodice back

Cut 4 (reverse 2)

↓
grain line

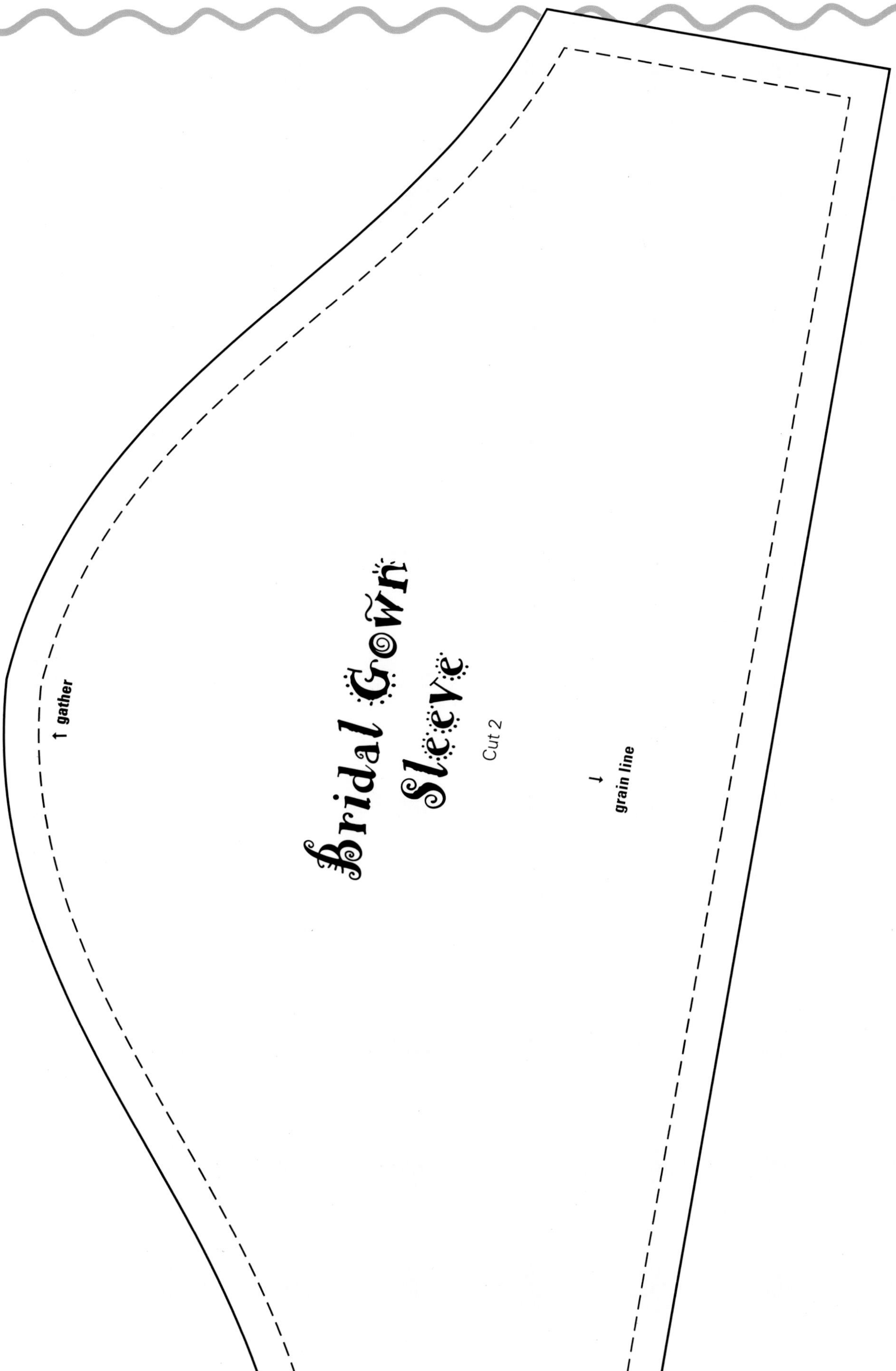

Bridal Gown
Sleeve

Cut 2

↑ gather

↓
grain line

You Are Invited...

An important element in every dollmaking class is interaction. Swapping ideas, seeking advice, sharing tips, and showing off finished dolls are all ingredients in the magical brew of a dollmakers' gathering.

In this spirit, let's share our dolls through the mail. Send photos and letters to me at the address below. Tell me about your dolls and yourself. Whether you use my patterns as is, modify them, or strike off with your own designs, I would enjoy meeting you and your dolls.

Jodie Davis

Jodie Davis Publishing, Inc.
15 West 26th Street
New York, NY 10010

or via email: CompuServe: 73522,2430
GEnie: J.DAVIS60

Sources

Carolee Creations

787 Industrial Drive
Elmhurst, IL 60126
Catalog: $2.00

Carolee's Sew Sweet dolls are just that. Many are soft sculpted from fleece fabric. Her catalog includes all supplies needed to construct the dolls.

CR's Crafts

Box 8
Leland, IA 50453
Catalog: $2.00 ($4.00 Canada)

Great prices and a wide selection of doll-and teddy bear–making supplies as well as general crafts supplies make this a must-have catalog. Dollmaking supplies include: plastic doll joints, stands, armatures, wigs (Lasioux new-born, 12 to 13 inches [30.4 to 33cm]), doll hair fibers, shoes, socks, tights, glasses, hats, plastic stuffing beads, dollmaker's needles, and quality fiberfill.

Dick Blick

P.O. Box 1267
Galesburg, IL 61401
Catalog: Free

Find the Berol Prismacolor 10% warm gray Art Marker, Pigma pens, colored pencils, crayons, fabric paint, and more for your dolls' faces in this huge art materials catalog.

Fleece & Unicorn

7th Avenue Center
123 West 7th Avenue #102
Stillwater, OK 74074-4029
Texture card: $3.00

My jaw dropped when I first saw these gorgeous yarns. The texture card has a sample of each yarn and lists the colors available.

Home Sew

Dept. JDP
Bethlehem, PA 18108
Catalog: Free

Low prices and great quantity prices on a limited selection of basic sewing supplies as well as laces, ribbons, and crafts supplies.

Keepsake Quilting

Dover Street
P.O. Box 1459
Meredith, NH 03253
Catalog: Free ($1.00 for first class mail)

Along with an excellent selection of quilting supplies, you will find doll patterns, books, the Stuff-It tool, Pigma pens, and muslin for doll bodies. For doll clothing, send for the swatch samples of cotton fabrics.

Mimi's books and Supplies

P.O. Box 662
Point Pleasant, NJ 08742

Contact Mimi to order a premade armature for the doll in chapter 3.

Patterncrafts

P. O. Box 25639
Colorado Springs, CO 80936-5639
Catalog: Free

A color catalog of doll and stuffed animal patterns, wearable art, the Stuff-It tool, and more.

Sax Arts & Crafts

P.O. Box 51710
New Berlin, WI 53151

Pigma markers in colored and black sets as well as a comprehensive array of art supplies.

Stitch 'N Craft Supply

5634 W. Meadowbrook
Phoenix, AZ 850031

Join this wholesale club to save on books, notions, quilting supplies, and a whole lot more. This is where you will find fancy threads such as the Madeira thread I used for satin stitching the edges of the appliqued clothing on one of my Basic Dolls.

Yarns

1 Mendon Street
Uxbridge, MA 01569

This is the source for the Ironstone mohair I used for the bride doll. Call or write to request information.

Bibliography

books

Bailey, Elinor Peace. *Mother Plays With Dolls*. McLean, Va.: EPM Publications, Inc., 1990.

Cely, Antonette. *Cloth Dollmaking*. This self-published three-ring binder is an excellent advanced text. Her dolls are convincingly lifelike. For information write to Antonette at 3692 Cherokee Rd., Atlanta, GA 30340-2749.

Davis, Jodie. *Easy-To-Make Cloth Dolls and All The Trimmings*. Charlotte, Vt.: Williamson Publishing Company, 1991.

_____. *Easy-To-Make Fairytale Characters and All the Trimmings*. Charlotte, Vt.: Williamson Publishing Company, 1993.

Dee, Diane Patterson. *The Cloth Dollmaker's Sourcebook*. White Hall, Va.: Betterway Publications, Inc.

Dodge, Venus A. *The Dolls*

Dressmaker. New York, N.Y.: Sterling Publishing, Inc., 1991.

Gourley, Miriam. *Cloth Dolls: How To Make Them.* Gualala, Ca.: The Quilt Digest Press, 1991.

Magazines

The Cloth Doll, P.O. Box 2167, Lake Oswego, OR 97035.

Dollmaker's Journal, 2900 West Anderson Lane, #20-150, Austin, TX 78757.

index